Ghostwriting

Aber Creative Writing Guides

Ghostwriting

Kate Walker's 12 Point Guide to Writing Romance

Starting to Write

The Business of Writing

The Craft of Fiction

Writing and Imagery

Writing Crime Fiction

Writing Historical Fiction

Writing How-to Articles and Books

Writing Science Fiction

Writing Soap

Writing TV Scripts

Aber Self-Help

Choose Happiness: Ten Steps to Put the Magic Back into your Life

Write yourself well: How writing therapy can help to cure emotional and physical pain

Aber Money Management

Understanding the numbers: the first steps in managing your money

Back to the Black: How to get out of Debt and Stay out of Debt

Aber publishing

Ghostwriting

How to Write for Others

Lynne Hackles

www.aber-publishing.co.uk

Disclaimer

The advice given in this book is given in good faith. However readers are advised, where appropriate, to obtain the services of suitably qualified professionals for advice, particularly when pertaining to legal matters. Neither the author nor the publisher nor any/all of its agents can be held responsible for any outcomes that result from the reading of this book.

Contents

Acknowledgements

I'd like to say a big thank you to everyone I've hassled whilst writing this book. That includes ghostwriters and my husband. Special thanks to Lynne Barrett-Lee, Anna Bowles, Chriss McCallum, Zoe King, Julia Anderson, Janie Jackson and Fiona Kendall and the other ghostwriters who contributed but wish to remain anonymous. You know who you are. I'd also like to thank the Freelance Hack from Writers' Forum and Martin Hodges.

Introduction

How this book will help

After much research, poking around, asking many people many questions and generally being a nuisance I am ready to share with you all the knowledge I have gleaned, together with my own personal experiences, and those of other ghostwriters.

You will discover that there are far more openings for ghostwriters than you may think. Ghostwriters have been used in the past for writing autobiographies, books and speeches but the market is expanding every day, thanks to the internet, and ghosts are everywhere, busily clicking away at keyboards, writing everything from adverts, poetry, articles, novels, children's books, memoirs and celebrity life stories.

Every day new markets for ghostwriting appear on the internet. It's becoming big business and there's no reason why you shouldn't have a piece of it. One statistic I found suggests that as many as forty percent of books have been ghosted. Another, according to publishing experts, stated that almost half of the titles of the New York Times bestsellers had been ghosted.

Any book that you pick up, on any subject, could have been ghostwritten. Actually, that is true for any printed material.

Definition of a ghostwriter

Put simply a ghostwriter writes and then gives credit of authorship to another. A ghostwriter is paid to write books, articles or whatever else their client wants. Ghostwriters are also asked to tidy up other people's work to make it ready for publication, or to do the research for a client's work and then write it up for them. Some ghostwriters learn to write in the style of a well-known author so they can produce books for that author.

Once the work is done the ghostwriter steps into the background and the work appears under the name of the client.

I managed to find ghostwriters who were happy to pass on tips, advice, warnings and anecdotes about their work. Some of them are named but others, due to the material, personal preference or confidentiality clauses in contracts, asked not to have their names used, therefore I have given them numbers. e.g. Ghost 1, Ghost 2 etc.

Ghostwriting is not purely for written work. Ghosts have been, and are, employed in the music business too. But this book is not about music. It's about us because writing is a skill we have, a job we do or a hobby we enjoy so why not share our skills and help others by writing their stories and non-fiction for them?

Why you need this book

Times are tough. Everyone says so. Life is becoming ever more difficult for writers. Publishers aren't taking risks on new novelists; markets for short stories are dwindling. If your income has dropped in recent years then you might consider taking up ghostwriting. It needn't be your full-time writing work and it needn't be life stories or full length pieces.

There are many forms of ghostwriting. Writing the life stories of celebrities is the tip of the iceberg. It may be the top tip but there's plenty of iceberg out of sight and this is the area a competent writer can slide into.

You are probably reading this book because you are already a writer. That's good. If you are a competent writer then you can become a ghostwriter. It doesn't matter if you are a poet, journalist, novelist or writer of short stories, there will be a form of ghostwriting to suit you.

How far you go depends on what you want. I ghost occasionally. Some writers develop ghostwriting as a business and it becomes the main part of their writing life. You can dip in your toe or dive in headfirst. It's up to you.

The great thing about ghosting is that you, as the ghostwriter, get paid whether the work is published or not.

Someone else's shoes

Can you step into someone else's shoes, live someone else's life? Does that sound scary? Think again. Fiction writers do it all the time. If you've written short stories or novels you've already stepped into someone else's shoes, into their skin. How do you think your main characters came to life? You invented those characters. That was the difficult part. You had to make them come alive on the page. You gave them problems, emotions, partners, children, jobs … With ghosting, your character is already there for you, fully formed and they arrive with all their own settings, cast of characters and even the plot. Isn't that less work?

Non-fiction

Have you written non-fiction? Articles? Reports? Magazine features? There are people out there who would love to do that. They have the information, the know-how, at their fingertips but they can't put it together for themselves. That's when a ghostwriter steps in.

Many people have to get their businesses, or themselves, out there and they use blogs, websites, Facebook and Twitter etc. to do so. Don't imagine for one moment that a busy celebrity is going to spend hours a day writing the content for these openings themselves. Or that an MP always writes all of his own speeches. Of course they don't. A ghost does it for them. You may not catch a celebrity as a client, though it's not impossible. It will probably be the man in the street who will turn up asking for help. Sounds boring? No. Everyone has a story to tell and you'd be amazed at what can happen to so called *ordinary* people.

Interested?

This book will be of use if you consider yourself to be a competent writer. More use if you can write quickly. It's for the writer who is not afraid to tackle anything and is always on the lookout for extra openings to write for, and to make money by doing so.

Ghosting is simply another string to the writer's bow, giving another opportunity to write and to make money. It is also a way of helping others—the ones who cannot or do not want to write their own life stories, articles, blogs …

Later I'll explain how to set yourself up as a ghostwriter, how to find work, and what sort of work is available. The quick answer to the latter question being all sorts of work. Long and short work, fiction and non-fiction will all be covered in these pages.

Ghostwriting is no longer swept under the carpet. It's nothing to be ashamed of and, judging by the number of ghostwritten best-sellers, it looks as if it is to play a large part in the future of the book trade and you could be a part of that future.

1 The job interview

The job description

What is a ghostwriter? Nearly all writers will understand the term 'ghostwriter'. Many of the reading public will not. When I told one person of my latest project, ghostwriting a story for someone, they became quite excited and told me they loved ghost stories. Ghostwriting has nothing to do with sitting in haunted houses or graveyards all night and then writing up what you may have seen, or hoped you'd seen. There are no old warriors carrying their heads under their arms. No rattling chains. No hauntings or exorcisms.

Make a note – Ask a few non-writing friends if they know what a ghostwriter is, and does.

A writer is a ghost when they are the invisible entity behind the work being promoted. You write something for a client and they get the credit. Their name is on the book, the story, the article, the blog. Your client gets all of the publicity. You may be allowed to stand around trying to blend into the bookshelves at signings, or you may not. Some clients won't allow it.

Your client provides the interviews for magazines, newspapers, radio and television. They may have needed your help before an interview. 'What shall I say if they ask me this, that or the other?' Your job may not finish with the publication of the book. Ghosts may often be needed to provide advice and even moral support for a client but you will remain in the background. As their ghost you write the work, take the money and keep quiet. Nothing spooky about that!

A ghostwriter is someone who can provide a professional service, write the work, and step back to allow the client to take the credit. To do that you need to enjoy writing for its own sake and not be the type who wants to write in order to be famous.

The first ghostwriters

Ghostwriting has been an occupation possibly since writing began.

There's a conspiracy theory over who wrote Shakespeare's plays. Could country-boy Will really have written them himself? Wasn't Stratford a bit out of the way of happening society in his day? How could a country bumpkin know such details of the places he wrote about? Many names have been put forward as probable authors. Possible contenders include men who were well travelled and educated, such as Edward de Vere, Ben Jonson, Christopher Marlowe or the Earl of Oxford. Perhaps William actually wrote the plays himself and there was no ghost involved.

Auguste Jules Maquet was a ghostwriter. He appeared to be happy with the role to begin with but, after arguments about money, he ended up in court with his writing partner. Here's a clue to who Auguste ghosted for. In the cemetery of Paris' Père-Lachaise the words engraved on his tombstone read—*The Three Musketeers*, *The Count of Monte Cristo* and *La Reine Margot*. There is a theory that Monsieur Maquet was responsible for the text of *The Three Musketeers* but he couldn't get it published as he was not a name. Nothing changes! That's when Alexander Dumas stepped in. He was already a well-known author but was always in debt. Maquet's masterpiece was, apparently, published under Dumas's name and so a lucrative relationship began. Both were writers but, while Dumas took the glory, Maquet remained the ghost.

Both of the examples given—Shakespeare and Dumas—have been the subject of furious debates. Were their works ghosted? Or did the men named actually produce their own work? Maybe we will never know for sure.

Up until a few years ago ghosting was a secret. Most of the population thought that books really were written by whoever's name was on the cover. Wrong! How can anyone who leads a full, busy life and has lots of commitments find the time to write their life story? The answer is they probably didn't. They hired a ghostwriter to do it for them. And now some of the ghosts are stepping into the limelight. Some ghosted authors even acknowledge that they had help with writing their book.

Many of us have heard of Andrew Crofts. He's a well-known ghostwriter. Isn't that an oxymoron? Well-known ghostwriter? It is because of his career that Andrew Crofts has become a name himself. He wrote *Sold*, for Zhana Musen, who, at the age of fifteen, was sold by her father and became a child bride. Andrew Crofts has ghosted many celebrity autobiographies including Jimmy Nail, Pete Bennett, the winner of the 2006 UK TV's *Big Brother* series, Melissa Bell who is the mother of *X Factor's* Alexandra Burke, Bette Davies, Gillian Taylforth … the list goes on. Both John Prescott and Paul Gascoigne had their life stories written by Hunter Davies. Katie Price (a.k.a. the model Jordan) managed multiple autobiographies and novels. Her ghost was Rebecca Farnworth.

Many of the public don't realise that celebrities' life-stories haven't been written by the celebrities pictured on the cover of the book, or indeed that novels written by celebrities are often written by an unknown name.

It has only been in recent times that ghosts have come out of 'the closet' and demanded to be noticed. Some have emerged to share a bit of the limelight, many still remain hidden, others are under contract to keep their secrets. Are you ready to join their ranks, even if it's only dipping in a toe? Read on and you'll discover how.

What does a ghostwriter do?

Ghostwriting is not limited to the glamorous or controversial life stories of celebrities. Ghosts write anything that clients want written. This could include letters, CVs, speeches, articles, fiction, life stories, single experiences, blogs, advertisements, poetry and a host of other things.

Ghostwriters make themselves available so that they can be easily contacted if anyone wants work done. Or they search out work for themselves by advertising their services and trawling through the internet opportunities. Due to the internet, the openings for ghostwriters are growing daily but should be checked thoroughly. Don't commit to a huge amount of work for an unspecified sum. Know exactly what you are expected to do and what the rewards will be.

In general, ghostwriters, especially new ones, need to put themselves out there in order to find work. This is the time when you do not want to be invisible.

Why ghostwriters are needed

Today we like to think that most of the population is literate but that's not true. Many still leave school unable to read or write well enough to write their own story. Some of these may go on to live interesting and useful lives and might, one day, want to have their experiences written down. They'd need a ghostwriter.

Of all the people who can read and write many would be stumped when it came to writing anything more creative than a shopping list or a thank-you letter. In truth, the last time many people wrote more than a page or two was during their schooldays but that doesn't stop them from having ideas. If they had an idea for a short story, a novel, or wanted to write their life story, they might turn to a ghostwriter for help.

Many years ago my children used to receive letters from their grandmother. She wanted to keep in touch as we lived miles away but she couldn't express herself in writing. When one of her letters arrived we all knew what it would say before even opening the envelope. They were all the same, practically word for word. We joked about her photocopying them and popping the top one off the pile into an envelope each week. When we visited she had lots of stories to tell her grandchildren. She could tell tales but had convinced herself that she wasn't capable of writing them down.

It seems easy for us to put down our thoughts on paper but we are the gifted ones—the writers. So many people have stories to tell and cannot get the words onto paper, or screen. Examples include:

- Violet was bombed out of her home during the war, joined the WAAF and learned how to control barrage balloons.
- Dennis was a Bantam, a regiment of soldiers who failed to reach the regulation height of 5 feet 3 inches. He fought and was wounded during WWI and his adventures died with him.

So many ordinary people have overcome extraordinary problems and lived difficult, joyful and interesting lives. Yes, it's said that everyone has a book in them and it is often true. We all have the book of our life. The fact is that many people would like their life story written and have great stories to tell but for one reason or another cannot write them for themselves. These are stories the following generations will enjoy reading. There's a huge interest in genealogy, researching the past, building family trees. Almost everyone wants to know where they have come from and what has made them the person they are. Maybe there isn't enough for a book but there's sufficient information for some nostalgic articles for a specialist magazine, a genealogy magazine or for one of the grey market magazines—those aimed at the over 50s.

This is where our writing talents are highly valued. If they can't write their own stories we can do it for them.

There's a difference between knowing what you want to say and having the ability to put the words on to paper. For example:

- A young man is asked to be best man at his friend's wedding. He knows how much this friendship has meant, he has some funny anecdotes he wants to tell the guests but when he sits down to actually write his speech he doesn't know where to begin. He needs a ghostwriter.
- A young woman has suffered a terrible ordeal but has survived and wants to tell the nation, the world, about her experiences. English was her worst subject at school and she has no idea how to get her emotions down in black and white. She needs a ghostwriter.

I met a woman who asked me how to set out a manuscript she had ready to send to a publisher. 'I sent so-and-so a proposal,' she said, 'and they asked to see the whole book.' What she told me next was staggering. She had sent the proposal to the publisher twenty-years ago. I didn't think the publishers she mentioned would remember her or her idea after such a long time. When I asked why she had taken so long she admitted to loving her subject but hating the writing part. She really should have asked a ghostwriter for help as soon as the company had expressed interest in her proposal.

> **Make a note** – Take pen and paper and quickly list as many friends' or relatives' interesting stories as you can think of. Give yourself five minutes. Then ask yourself if those involved would want their stories written up and, if sold, split the money with you.

Busy, busy

If someone else has the knowledge but not the know-how then a ghost can write up their specialist subjects for them. For instance:

- A successful business man wants to write his life story, and is quite capable of doing so, if only he had the time.
- A therapist wants to write about his or her profession and impart knowledge to others.

Both need a ghostwriter. Just because you've never owned a dog doesn't mean you can't write a short book about a specific breed. If your diet is chocolate, crisps and assorted junk food it doesn't prevent you from writing articles on healthy nutrition. Your clients give you the information and you put down the words.

Lots of people with stories to tell about their lives, beliefs, businesses or experiences are too busy to ever get around to sitting down for long enough to write a book. They may not have the time or inclination to write it themselves but would dearly love to see a book about their business or their special expertise whether it be how to run a hotel or their take on positive thinking. And they'd like to see their name on it. They have the information to impart but not the skills to do so. What can they do? Look for someone with those skills. That's us! They hire a ghost to write it for them.

Can't write, won't write

Others know they can't put pen to paper. They don't have the vocabulary to express themselves. Watch a TV personality being interviewed and often you can tell for yourself. Count how many times *basically* crops up in the conversation, or *you know what I mean*. They may talk in clichés but we don't write in them, do we? Well, maybe we would if we were using their voices but we'd try to make them sound more intelligent and we'd edit the repetition of those well-worn phrases.

The job interview

Could you be a ghost? Unless you are a disappointed member of the public who was expecting to find the story of a ghost in these pages who, when not haunting, spent their spare time writing, I'm guessing you are already a writer. Perhaps you write in a genre—crime fiction, romance, historical sagas, or maybe you write the short stuff—features, articles, stories. If you are not published yet, or if you have a CV stretching over several sheets of A4 then you could branch out, try something a little different and ghost. If you are unpublished up to now, this might prove to be your forté. Any writer who can get inside a character or empathise with other members of the human race can be a ghost. Any writer who enjoys learning about new things can be a ghost. Answer the following questions to see if you are ghostwriter material.

- Can you write?
- Can you write quickly?
- Are you the sort of writer who says yes first and thinks later?
- Are you prepared to tackle anything?
- Are you interested in people?
- Are you interested in learning new things?

If you answered yes to most of the above then you're halfway there.

Can you write?

Obviously you will need to be able to. You will need the skills that many of the public have never learned or forgotten—good grammar, punctuation, a clear and precise way of expressing yourself.

> **Make a note** – If you aren't one hundred per cent sure of your punctuation or grammar then buy a good book on the subject (*Perfect Grammar* Derek Soles, Studymates).

Can you write quickly?

Writing quickly is a great advantage. Some jobs might be needed yesterday. Others will be required as soon as possible. Life stories may take months but the sooner you tackle the job and complete it the sooner you'll be able to start on the next project.

Are you the sort of writer who says yes first and thinks later?

Most serious writers can't afford to turn down work. Many writing friends of mine say yes automatically when asked to write something/anything. Look before you leap doesn't apply when you write for money/a living.

I have always said yes to anything offered me. Sometimes there have been regrets. Not often. When starting out I used to say that even if the writing was needed in Swahili the answer would be yes. The problem could be tackled later.

Are you prepared to tackle anything?

There are subjects I would say no to, pornography being one of them. If you suffer from arachnophobia and are asked to write a book for an expert on spiders then it might make sense to say no. On the other hand tackling the subject could be a way of dispersing your fear.

If it's legal, ethical and interesting, then go for it. You cannot be afraid. Being afraid takes away much of the fun.

Make a note – List the subjects you would not want to write about. What offends you? What would you not be comfortable with?

Are you interested in people?

Writers tend to be interested in people. They are the ones on the sidelines at parties. Writers can be chatty but when a new character (person) enters their lives then they will be the ones asking all the questions. Writers need to know what makes non-writers tick. They see someone waiting at a bus stop and wonder where they are going, why they are alone and what's in their bag. They overhear one line of conversation and want to know all the details. Writers want to know about other people's lives, their loves, successes, failures, children, jobs … In short, are you nosey? Or if you prefer, are you inquisitive?

Are you interested in learning new things?

Writers are told to write what they know but that doesn't prevent them from learning new things. Long ago I was asked to write a property column for a local newspaper. Fortunately I was working in a building society at the time so when the manager went out for lunch I'd nip into his office and sift through his paperwork for any snippets that could be used. It wasn't long before I became an almost-expert on mortgages, insurances and the housing market in general. Learning new things means contacting experts, researching, and reading. None of those are impossible, or even difficult. If a bee-keeper has been asked to write about his business and then asks you to do it for him you do not say no because all you know about bees is that they have yellow and black stripes and they sting. Your client will give you the information you need, or hopefully most of it and research will do the rest. Don't be put off by the small stuff, such as lack of knowledge. Knowledge can be acquired and it can be fantastically interesting to hear how reflexology works, how women fought for the vote, how you can make a hundred and one things with lavender, the history of the bicycle. Subjects you may never have given a thought to might turn out to be completely absorbing.

The skills a ghostwriter needs

You already have the ability to write. What you may need to cultivate are interviewing skills. We will cover more on this in Chapter 5. You will also have to sound and look like a professional. Don't go meeting clients looking as if you've just crawled out of bed. Check in the mirror before leaving. Does that reflection look like someone you would tell your life secrets to, or employ to write a self-help manual, or an engineering one?

If you are nervous, do as I do, and use the '*As If*' principle. You act as if you are confident, capable, and successful. It works. Trust me. I've been doing it for years.

Remember that your client is likely to be as nervous as you are. Part of your job is to put them at their ease so that they will confide in you, and trust you. They need you to be professional, assured and in control. If this is difficult, take a deep breath and chant to yourself, 'Relaxed, cool, calm and in control.' It's what I used to do when I started out interviewing people.

What a ghostwriter doesn't need

Forget ego here. A ghostwriter is practically invisible and most are unknown. If you want to write subjects that appeal to you then ghostwriting is not the way to go. If you want to show off your work and sign books in big stores then ghostwriting isn't going to get that for you.

Working hard

The ability to work hard comes with practice. Take a few weeks off from writing and it's like beginning all over again when you get back to it. You feel rusty and aren't happy with what you produce but keep at it and those skills will return. Like riding a bicycle they cannot be forgotten.

> **Make a note** – to plan your day so that you have time to spend on promoting the ghostwriting side of your writing business, and also time to actually ghostwrite.

Don't wait for the Muse. She/he is always on holiday. When starting any project it's the initial start that is the most difficult. That blank page, the first step. Once you get going you'll wonder what the problem is. Trust me. I'm a writer.

Henry Ford was supposed to have said to his son, "The harder you work the luckier you get." Certainly the harder you work in the world of publishing the more your name gets around and that's exactly what you want.

When, as a young mother, I began writing the thought of the gas bill, school uniforms and new shoes always spurred me on to write and sell a story. A friend has just *written* a conservatory, in other words sold enough material to pay for the new conservatory on her home.

For Non-UK Readers: Many UK homes have a conservatory, it is a room that extends into the garden usually from the back of the home. It is largely made from glass and when the weather is too cold to sit out, can be a great way of enjoying light and sunshine.

If thinking money helps, then be materialistic. There's no need to tell anyone that you are. Let them think it's all down to love and inspiration and not just the filthy lucre.

The shock factor

Books have been ghosted about child abuse, paedophilia, gory real-life murders, and even incest. You name it and someone has been on the receiving end. Many of these sufferers, victims or perpetrators want to write about their experiences. If they approach you then you have to give some thought to whether you would want to tackle their subject, or not. If it's going to shock you, offend you, or is against your moral principles then think again. You have the right to say no. ('It's very kind of you to ask me but I have to say no thank-you,' if it's a murderer.)

The first book I ghosted was half-written when my subject dropped a bomb-shell. Her husband had been involved in something highly illegal, immoral and heart-breaking. What was I to do? Forfeit all the time, work and effort put into the project or act like a professional journalist and get on with the job? I decided on the latter. The details were uncomfortable to listen to, and were even more uncomfortable to write up but the book was completed and it was my client's story, warts and all. She deserved ten out of ten for her complete, and often brutal, honesty.

Profile of a good ghostwriter

So we have established the profile of a good ghostwriter. They have an insatiable curiosity about people, places, and of course subjects. They enjoy writing and can do so proficiently. They are unafraid and they love to write. Does that sound remotely like you? Even if you lack a couple of the above attributes they can soon be learned with practice and experience.

I have a writing friend who would make an excellent ghostwriter. She is interested in people. She asks questions when she meets someone new. She remembers their name. She has a great curiosity about everyone. Meet up with her after any length of time and you are likely to be interrogated.

Another string to your bow

In the world of freelancing it's not good to be reliant on one or two markets. Magazine editors change, and people's needs change. In recent years many women's' magazines have stopped using fiction. General interest magazines are using staff to provide features. It's always good to have money arriving from several different directions instead of relying on one or two outlets. Branch out as a professional writer. Try writing genres you've not tried before. They could surprise and stimulate you, and ghostwriting could be one of them.

It's worth remembering that a ghost will get paid for their work whether it gets into print or not. You decide on a price and put together a contract before beginning. See Chapter 4. Selling and being paid for work you write without being commissioned is a gamble and may not bring in any wages. Ghostwriting will and it can be done alongside any regular work you have, or while you are writing your, hopefully, best-selling novel.

'I love that I can apply my skills at narrative writing to bring someone's story to life, and I love that they love what I do for them. It's also a lot more reliable as a means of earning a living than fiction writing seems to be right now. That said, I'm working on another novel too.'

Lynne Barrett-Lee
www.lynnebarrett-lee.com

So, if you write for a living or simply to make a bit of extra money then ghostwriting is another outlet for your work. All you need to do is find the outlets and the clients which means setting up your own business. Chapter Two will tell you how to go about it.

> Make a note – If you are serious about ghostwriting then, like a good reporter, you need to be always on the lookout for a good story.

Ghostwriting opportunities

These are a few of the opportunities you should be looking out for when it comes to building up a business. All of the following may need a ghostwriter.

- A celebrity who wants their autobiography written.
- An *ordinary* person who wants their autobiography, or memoirs, written.
- An *ordinary* person who has a story to tell.
- A blogger who wants their posts to be entertaining and informative.
- A professional who wants their specialised subject written but can't do it for themselves.
- A website owner who wants to be noticed but doesn't know what to write.
- Anyone who has to give a speech but feels intimidated.
- A celebrity who has an idea for a novel.
- An *ordinary* person who has an idea for a novel.
- A young man who wants a romantic poem for his girl-friend, or vice-versa.
- A publisher who wants a book, or books, written by a ghost for an author who does not exist.
- A company who want their products written about, advertised, or blogged about.
- Someone living locally who has local knowledge about places, personalities, buildings etc. but does not have the ability to write it up for themselves.

Points to remember

- If you can write you can ghostwrite.
- There is a huge market for ghostwriters.
- Everyone has a story but not everyone can write their story.
- Stretching yourself by tackling different subjects will improve your writing and your CV.

2 Setting up a business

Sucking eggs

First of all, my apologies if you have read this before, in so many places, and know what you are doing. However I do ask you to have patience and consider this short section a recap on what you need to have in order to work.

Even if ghostwriting is only going to be a small part of your writing life you will still need to be professional about it. Consider it a business. Luckily it's one that can be started with very little financial commitment. You probably already have everything you need.

The tools to work with

Unless you're a complete beginner you will already have a computer with internet connection. You will also have all the other apparatus a writer needs in order to work—a telephone, printer, paper, spare inkjets or printer ink cartridges, pens, a filing system.

You also need exposure, writing skills, clients, and an ability to work hard. As a writer you no doubt already have all the aforementioned but you might want to add a tape recorder, preferably a digital one, to your shopping list. They come in very useful when interviewing clients.

> **Make a note** – Start a shopping list and make sure you have everything you need.

A place to work

You'll also need an office. When I say office you don't have to rush out and rent one. Office loosely means a space in which to write. I need to be shut away from all distractions but some friends can write in crowded rooms, cafés, on trains. You might even manage to get your ghosting done while you commute to work on the train. If, like me, you need a place to call your own, then find one sharpish. A corner of a bedroom, a space at the top of the stairs, in the attic or the basement, a summerhouse, shed, anywhere you can shut yourself away and get useful chunks of alone-time. Even if you always write on the sofa, or during breaks at your "proper" job, you will still need somewhere to store your notes.

> **Make a note** – It's always a good idea to tidy up your office space before beginning a new project.

A place to interview clients

Should it be your place or theirs? Or somewhere neutral?

If you propose interviewing your clients from your own home you will need to think about a comfortable space in which you can do so. From your point of view this is probably the easiest way for you to work.

In the early stages of your relationship with your client it's a good idea to have someone else in the house with you. Maybe you could ask your partner/sister/whoever to answer the door to your client. This will let your client know that you are not alone.

Don't go inviting clients into a messy room where books and papers have to be moved before you can sit down. Make your interviewing space relaxing because, unless the client is relaxed, you won't get the best out of them. Make them welcome. Make them comfortable. Make them a cup of tea. Then ask questions or, better still, allow them to do the talking.

> **Make a note** – You will need to decide which part of your home you are going to use for interviews. Keep it tidy and make sure you and your client are not interrupted.

With some clients your home could be the wrong venue. There are ghostwriters who hire a hotel room and spend several days with their client and, over that period of time, glean all the information they need to complete the task. This, of course, isn't always possible. Costs need to be considered.

Other clients could feel happier being interviewed in their own office, especially if the commission is to write about their business or their rise to wealth and fame. If they are busy people they may prefer that.

For short ghosting jobs such as speeches or short articles a café might suit the purpose. Do remember though that a voice recorder will pick up all the background noise and there's a chance that, once back at your desk, the tape turns out to be useless.

Selling your services

The one time when ghostwriters need to be up front and visible is when it comes to selling their services. Exposure is the word.

You will definitely need a website and a blog and if you are the type who can go on Twitter or Facebook for short periods of time, as opposed to spending those chunks of alone-time messing about on them, then go for those too. Online writing forums are another opportunity for you to promote your ghostwriting business.

Websites

Websites need to be kept updated. Some clients may allow you to feature the work you did for them and this can be your shop window. You could also offer to sell clients' books via your website. Write up a current CV and add that to your site. List all the work you have done but, if your client has sworn you to secrecy, make sure you are not specific when describing the job you did for them. Above all make sure your website looks professional. Triple check for grammar or spelling mistakes. Then ask someone else to check too. Would you trust a ghost if you checked out their website and found it full of typos, poor grammar and incorrect spelling?

A client who wanted help to write her story came to me via my website. At the time I had not actually mentioned on it that I would take on ghostwriting projects but a book I'd ghostwritten was mentioned there. One of my hobbies was also listed and that was the reason why she chose me. We shared the same interest so she thought I would be the perfect ghost for her.

It would be worth listing some of your hobbies and interests in an About Me section. You never know who might come along requiring your ghosting services because of your passion for making potpourri or your addiction to hang-gliding. You should definitely include any areas that you are an expert in.

> **Make a note** – If you haven't got a website and don't have the technical know-how to set one up for yourself then look for someone who can do it for you. Try family and friends before you start searching for someone who will want to be paid.

> **Make a note** – If you are serious and want ghostwriting work then you must let everyone know. Check your website and make sure you are telling everyone that you are available for such work. Make it easy for them to contact you by providing a link so they can email you.

Emails

Add a signature to all your emails offering your ghostwriting services. You can do this by clicking on Tools, then Options, Signatures and New. Then type in what you want to say, tick Add to all outgoing messages. Apply. OK and it's done. Do remember to update your signature when necessary. Delete the service if you are busy with other work and not actively looking for ghostwriting projects.

Also add to the end of your emails any books you want to sell on behalf of clients.

Contact everyone in your address book and let them know about your ghostwriting services.

Traditional advertisements

If you prefer more traditional methods of getting your business known then place a few advertisements in appropriate magazines. For instance, if you fancied writing life stories for older people try any of the 'grey market' magazines, that is those aimed at the over 50s. Writing magazines also carry adverts for writing services such as proof-reading, researching and ghostwriting.

Produce a postcard-sized advertisement to display wherever you are allowed. Some supermarkets have boards on which local businesses can display their wares. Libraries have notice boards for events, clubs, and services. Lookout for any opportunities.

Make a note – Let other libraries in the area know about your ghostwriting business, not only the one nearest to you. Decide on the size of area you are prepared to cover. How far are you willing to travel?

Business cards

Make sure you always carry your business cards wherever you go. Have all your contact details on them and list your services. If you already list yourself as a freelance writer and creative writing tutor then get a new batch with ghostwriter added. Don't ever be caught without your business cards to hand. Keep a few in handbags, pockets, shopping bags. Wherever you go, be sure to take your cards with you.

Keep them clear and to the point. Avoid fancy fonts that might be difficult to read. Don't try to be clever and add pictures, especially those little inkpots and quills so favoured by writers who have never used, or seen, them in the flesh. Make your card clear, simple, and precise.

> **Make a note** – to get business cards printed. Keep them clear and to the point. You are offering ghostwriting services.

Local newspapers

Once you have a ghostwriting commission, or two, under your belt, try contacting the local newspapers to ask if they'd be interested in interviewing you. Ghostwriting sounds so intriguing that they are unlikely to turn down your request.

Press releases

Sending out a Press Release is a free way of getting your news out there. First of all you will need some news. It's unlikely that a newspaper would use a press release about you setting up in business as a ghostwriter but if you have a particular item of news then let all the local papers know about it. An event would make a good subject so if you are giving a talk then let the paper know and tell them it is about you being a ghostwriter.

Journalists will read the press releases they receive and write them up as news items. If you've done a good job and not produced too many words, your release may go into the paper unaltered, but it's more than likely that it will be cut and edited in order to fill a gap.

Write a Press Release for yourself and send it out to every newspaper, local magazine and radio station in whatever area you feel comfortable working within; ten, twenty, fifty, a hundred mile radius. It's up to you.

A press release should say exactly what it is at the top of the page. Then come up with something attention grabbing. In the body of the release give all the information a newspaper might need. Make it interesting enough and you could get a phone call and be asked for more information, or a photograph.

At the bottom of your press release put the date it can be released. For instance, the day before the book mentioned is on sale, or a week before you give your talk. If your news isn't date specific then put *For immediate release*. This should be followed by all your contact details—name, address, phone (home and mobile), email, fax. Make sure there's no excuse for them not being able to contact you. Keep to one side of A4. Journalists are busy people.

Here's an example of a Press Release.

Press Release
Sandra Smith
I'm A Ghost!

For one night only Sandra Smith is going to reveal herself to the public. Sandra is a ghost. She has been seen haunting book shops when book signing events are taking place but Sandra never does the signing. You won't find her name on any book spine. Sandra is a ghostwriter. Her clients supply the stories but she writes the words.

'Being a ghostwriter means I get to cover many lives,' says Sandra, 'and at this talk I will be covering some of the subjects I've written about.' These include several interesting life stories, a book on Feng Shui written on behalf of an expert in the subject, and a best-selling novel which has the name of a famous actress on its cover.

Sandra will be talking about *My Life As A Ghost* at The Studio Theatre, Any Street, Any Town, at 8pm on Thursday 4th August.

Tickets are available from the box office. Prices from £x.
ends
For immediate release.

Any additional information required please contact Mrs Sandra Smith, address, telephone numbers, fax, email.

Make a note – Write your own press release and list all of the places you can think of to send it out to.

Radio stations

A Press Release can be sent to radio stations. Local stations are always looking out for interesting personalities and that means you—the ghostwriter. Once again, the listeners will be intrigued to know what a ghost does. The very word *ghost* will interest the public enough to tune in. What could be more interesting than a ghost on air? You can be sure the station would milk that word for all its worth.

Talks

As a writer, have you given talks? This is another way to get out there and let people know you are offering a service. Offer a talk to the Writers' Circles in your area. Women's Institutes, Probus Clubs, all sorts of clubs and societies are on the lookout for entertaining speakers. Talk to a group about ghostwriting and there may be someone in the audience who needs your services. Nearly every member of that audience will go home and tell another person about you. And so your fame spreads. Word gets around and jobs begin to trickle in.

My first client—a personal experience

My first client found me via a library and writers' group. Let's call her Susan. She had a kiss-and-tell tale to tell and wanted someone to write it for her. She knew that it was beyond her capabilities so began looking for help. She called in at her local library and asked if they knew of any ghostwriters. They didn't but they did point her in the direction of the local Writers' Circle. Susan was given the secretary's phone number. When she contacted her she was told they didn't have anyone experienced enough to take on the job. (They probably did but no-one was prepared to be brave and try something new.) They suggested another group she could contact and gave her a number. That number was mine.

Make a note – Let other writing groups in your designated area know about your ghostwriting skills and that you are prepared to take on work.

The Three-Foot-Rule

There's a sales ploy called the Three-Foot-Rule. I learned about it on a visit to one of those big American companies who tell you it's possible to earn thousands in your spare time by selling their product.

The Three-Foot-Rule has not been changed into metric because the Metre Rule doesn't have the same ring to it. The Three Foot Rule means exactly what it says. Whenever you are within three feet of anyone you should be selling to them. The idea is that you chat—at a party, a bus stop, a doctor's waiting room—and mention the product you are selling. In this case ghostwriting services. As a writer I try steering the conversation around to jobs. Ask what they do and they'll respond, 'And you?' Then tell them you're a ghostwriter. If you say writer they'll want to know your name and ask if they should know you. As a ghostwriter they won't expect to know your name though you may have to explain the concept of ghostwriting to them.

In my experience, nine times out of ten, your new friend will tell you they have always wanted to write a book and most will add, "When I've got time." Ask what sort of book they want to write and, if it shows promise, offer to do it for them. Tell them how they'll have their name on the cover and, if they wish it, you will be sworn to secrecy. Then hand them your business card. Nothing may come of it but a small percentage may mull the suggestion over and contact you later. A small percentage is better than no percentage at all.

The Three-Foot-Rule is not for the faint-hearted and opportunities for bringing your product into the conversation can prove difficult. But when they do crop up make sure you are ready. Swallow your shyness and shamelessly promote yourself.

Agents and publishers

If, or when, you have a CV and can show examples of ghosted work you could try approaching agents and publishers. People who want books written sometimes approach an agent asking for help. If that agent knows about you, and your interests, you could pick up work. If no-one knows what you're doing you're not going to get anywhere.

Chriss McCallum tells her story.

'I was invited to a meeting in Manchester with about thirty other members of the Society of Authors. We'd come from quite a wide area and had all responded to an email from the Society asking if anyone was interested in ghostwriting. The meeting was arranged by an agent who'd had several requests from members of the public regarding finding ghostwriters. The agent was also working with some of the staff from the English department at Manchester University. Having registered an interest at the meeting, I was later approached by the agent and offered a ghostwriting commission.'

Journalist, Jane Bidder, says, 'I was approached by an expert who had been asked by a publisher to write a book on his speciality. He didn't have the time so, as I had interviewed him in the past, he asked the publisher if I could be his ghostwriter.'

'For my first project,' says Zoe King, 'I was approached because I was a member of The Society of Women Writers & Journalists.'

'I was working for a company offering correspondence courses for writers. When the company decided to offer a self-publishing service I was asked for help when they were approached by a Colonel who wanted someone to ghost his biography.'

Janie Jackson

Julia Anderson had a long wait before her first ghostwriting job. '*I had mentioned two decades ago that I would like one day to try my hand at ghostwriting,*' she says, '*and twenty years later I was asked to ghost a book. The person had spent fifteen years handwriting what turned out to be the bare bones of the story.*'

Lynne Barrett-Lee was approached by one of her husband's former patients. '*She'd read my work, and followed my weekly newspaper column,*' she says, '*and asked if I'd consider helping her write her life story.*'

Groups and organisations

If you are not already a member of any writing group or organisation then jump to it. There are requirements necessary for joining the Society of Authors or the Society of Women Writers and Journalists. You probably already have the qualifications to join one or the other. There are also other organisations which could prove helpful. See *The Writers' and Artists' Yearbook* (A&C Black) for more.

You find them, they find you

If you stick at advertising your ghostwriting services for long enough clients will eventually contact you. It's not easy setting up any new business and all take a while to establish. Persevere and keep telling everyone what you do and letting them know how to get in touch with you.

Networking

Most clients will come to you but there's no harm in going out and looking for some yourself. It's called networking. This means you need to get about, show yourself and meet other people who might be useful to you. Doesn't that sound awful? I prefer to think of networking as making new friends. It certainly can be.

When I began writing I joined a group, went to every workshop that was advertised locally, queued up in bookshops and libraries when authors were speaking, became a delegate at conferences and, using the 'As If' principle, I acted 'as if' I wasn't the least bit nervous about meeting these wonderful people who had achieved what I aspired to—being in print. I smiled and I spoke to them and can honestly say there wasn't one single author who turned away or couldn't be bothered to speak to me.

Don't network with writers only. As an aspiring ghost you need to network wherever you go. It could be the golf club, the supermarket queue, the garden centre ... the more people you meet, the more you can advertise that you are a ghostwriter and the better the chance is of getting commissions. Ghosts are supposed to be in the background once they have written a client's book. They may not even be invited to book signings if the client thinks they might give the game away. But ghosts do need to be very visible when looking for work.

'Because your would-be author is unlikely to know the vagaries of the publishing market, it is important that you as a ghostwriter keep abreast of developments within the industry. This is where networking is invaluable. Do as much as you possibly can, whether it's via writers' organisations such as SWWJ, The Society of Authors, etc., or via writers' conferences. Also, keep an eye on the writers' press, such as Writers' News and Writers' Forum.'

Zoe King
www.zoeking.com

Make a note – Network, network, network

Looking for clients

Everyone has a book in them. True or false? I think it's true because everyone has their own life experiences to write about. Some will be far more interesting than others but everyone's life is important to them and many people would like to see theirs written.

Looking for celebrities

Who do you know? Does someone famous live in your town? Have you met or are you going to meet someone who has performed in the theatre and been on a national tour, or appeared on television? Look out for opportunities to meet celebrities.

I appeared on a popular television game show, *Deal Or No Deal,* and thus became a celebrity, albeit for a short time. A writer contacted me asking if he could write up my story. Naturally, I had already sold it to several different magazines but, when I explained that I could write up my own experiences the writer generously gave me the contact address of the editor he had run the idea by and she agreed that I could write my own piece. If the writer had worked on my story it would have been an "*as told to*" piece, probably '*Lynne's Big Win, as told to Unnamed Freelance*'. But if I, or the unnamed freelance writer, had contacted a non-writer who had been on the show we could have written their experience for them and used their name. Either of us could have ghosted for them.

Perhaps a friend or acquaintance has won on *Lotto* or *Euromillions* or the lottery where you live. They will be in the news and classed, for a while, as a celebrity. There might be a good back-story to their win—such as them being bankrupted and losing their home just before winning—and you could be the ghost who writes up their experience.

This sort of news is often in the local newspaper. They report what has happened but you could turn it into a more interesting piece for a magazine by using the emotions, feelings and experiences of the person involved. This could be classed as an interview piece if you put your own name to it but many people, when asked, would prefer to see their name on it, and for others to think they had written it themselves.

Not many of us happen to live next door to a film star or a big name on television but you might know someone who knows someone. Keep those ears open and if your auntie tells you that her next door neighbour's son has starred in a West End production, ask if it would be possible to meet him. Who knows, he may be considering having his story written and you would appear in his life at the right moment. Luck often has to do with being in the right place at the right time.

Looking for everyday heroes

Once again you can find these stories in the local newspaper, or hear the news from others. *Local hero saves family from fire* reads the headline, and the facts of the story are there for all to read. It's a ghost's job to get inside the hero's thoughts and write an article for him, or maybe even a book.

> **Make a note** – Buy your local newspaper each week and check it out for possible ghostwriting jobs.

There will undoubtedly be hundreds of interesting people in your area, though they will certainly not be big names. Think of all the contacts you've made from all the differing areas of your life. Those involved in the same hobbies, sports, and interests as you. People who have achieved, who have suffered, overcome obstacles, cheated death.

Looking for family stories

I'm writing our family history for our grandson. Lots of grandparents want to do the same. Almost all the grandparents, and great-grandparents, you know might want their family history chronicled. I am capable of writing ours. Are they capable of writing theirs? The answer is probably not.

Lookout and listen to older people. My mother lived in sheltered housing and everyone there had a story to tell.

They had all survived the war for starters, but what other treasures lurked in their pasts?

My father-in-law was a train driver, a reserved occupation during the war. He thought he hadn't done his bit for King-and-Country but, years after he died, one of his friends told us how he had been carrying explosives when an air raid occurred. Without thinking what might happen to him he reversed his train until it was safely in a tunnel. Can you believe he had never thought to mention this to any of us?

There are lots of stories like my father-in-law's. They belong to the men and women in the street, ordinary people who don't consider that they've done anything out of the ordinary. They do not brag about their brave exploits but, if you can find them, they may tell you and allow you to write them up, whether it is for a magazine or a book. A collection of these stories could be interesting and it would be up to you to put the right words into the mouths of the contributors. You listen to their stories and then bring them alive.

All the unwritten stories

I had a friend called Christina. She had been the first female motorbike courier during the Second World War. I didn't know this until she died and it was mentioned at her funeral. Ever since I've wondered what stories she had to tell. Hopefully she told them to her children and grandchildren. It would be too awful if they died with her but how many people does this happen to?

Next time you're in a crowded town centre look around. Everyone you can see has a story.

- The mother with the severely disabled child may have formed a group for other parents struggling to cope, or be at the forefront of a charity raising money to research the problem her child was born with.
- The young man with the rucksack may be on a journey to walk around the world.

- The couple peering in the window of a cycle shop may be about to attempt to break the record for cycling from John O'Groats to Land's End.
- The woman being watched by the store detective could be suffering from a very real disease—kleptomania. Something others don't understand but you could enlighten them if you took on her story.

Sit and watch the passers-by for ten minutes. Potentially a good percentage of them would have stories worth writing, whether as a short article or a complete book. But the majority of those you see would not be able to write it for themselves. They'd need a ghost. You could do it for them.

> **Make a note** – Always be on the lookout for a story

Real life popularity

There is a theory that we are all interested in the real life stories that magazines are stuffed with, and which are all over our televisions screens, because so many of us do not have the old-fashioned family life—the support that families had years ago when all their relatives lived within walking distance of each other. We had someone to turn to in times of trouble, advice and help from folk who knew us. Nowadays the neighbours are strangers, faceless and nameless, yet characters on soaps are easily recognised and named. Soaps are popular because the soap families become real to the viewers who tune in to find out what's happening to them. The same goes for all the true life stories and shows. We like to see how others manage. We are interested in other people's lives but many of those people cannot write. Once again, this is where you step in as a ghostwriter. Reading about others' lives will never wane in popularity.

Insatiable appetite

For many years there have been predictions that the public were getting fed up with real life dramas. Sales of celebrity life-stories were going to drop. Has it happened? Check the television schedules to see how much reality they use. Cameras are positioned in family homes so we can watch how other people live. We hear how victims coped, or didn't, with accidents, war, natural disasters or attacks. Young adults reveal all their secrets to presenters like Jeremy Kyle, celebrities invite us into their lives to share their joys and woes. Doesn't all that prove that there is an insatiable appetite for real-life stories?

Browse the shelves of a bookstore, or the pages of a magazine, and you will see the proof that real life dramas are as popular as ever. There remains, and probably always will, a huge market for these stories. Whether they are ordinary, famous, brave, stupid or tragic the public continue to have an avid interest in real life stories. As humans we will always be interested in other humans and will always want to read articles or books about them. This is where the ghostwriter steps in.

You may not be able to sell a book to a major publisher but publishing just one copy of a book can easily be achieved now. Self-publishing is no longer expensive and can prove a solution to all the grandparents who want to leave their stories for their children, grandchildren and even later generations. If only a few copies are needed then it's possible to produce them on a computer, together with photographs.

Kiss-and-tell

Many celebrity features fall into this category. A relationship goes wrong and one party or the other, sometimes both, sell their story to a national newspaper. Some wronged partners even go as far as getting a book written. It's not only celebrities who do this. Many ordinary folk might want to wreak revenge through the printed word. Take care when considering whether to say yes to such a story as these are the ones that are likely to cause problems and could even lead to legal action. If you do go ahead make sure you have a clause in the contract that indemnifies you for all comments made by your client. In other words the client agrees that s/he takes full responsibility for any legal outcomes. Another thought is to register as a company since you will then have limited liability. This means that you would only be liable for the value of the company and would therefore, in the event of being sued, not risk losing your home. If you do become a company there are strict requirements in law placed on you so do take legal advice from an appropriate professional.

Online information

If you have a week or two to spare type "ghostwriting" into a search engine and scan your way through the tens of thousands of opportunities, but beware, many want you to work for peanuts. More on this in Chapter 8.

Convincing the public

Think of the product you are going to produce—a piece of ghostwritten work of some sort. How do you convince the public that they need this service?

Everyone wants their lives to run smoothly and easily. Most will tell you that there simply aren't enough hours in the day for them to do everything they need and want to. If they want to see their idea in print but don't have the time to do it themselves then you are giving them time together with a professional service which will enable their dreams to come true. The media put out the message that everything can be achieved quickly and easily—*Lose a Stone in Four Weeks, Stop smoking in five easy steps, learn to swim in one easy lesson.* See the important words here? *Easy* and *Simple* often feature. And the other draw is the few stages or short time span needed in order to realise your dream. This is what you will be offering to clients. You can make the writing of their book simple and possible for them to do without spending too much of their valuable time on it. You need to convince them that they cannot do without a ghostwriter.

You can also give the public compelling reasons to have their memoirs written for them. Genealogy is a popular hobby now. There are television programmes and magazines about it. There are websites. Who wouldn't want to know about their ancestors' lives? If I had a copy of my Great-grandmother's life story it would be something to treasure. As it is, I know very little about her. Imagine your great-grandchild being able to read about your life.

Memoirs make wonderful gifts for the family and will be kept for generations. By helping someone write their memoirs you are enabling them to leave such a gift. The information in them will help make sense of the family tree. It will also create a little bit of personal and social history.

A radio interview

Here's part of a ghostwriter's interview. See how they get their skills across and how they persuade the listener—this was on radio—that they need her services.

Q: What sort of person hires a ghostwriter?

A: Many of your listeners might want to write their life stories, or have an idea for a novel but not a clue as to how to start. My clients are often the types who didn't like writing at school and still don't like to write. They are also busy people who might have the skills to write their own books or articles but can't find the time and, even if they could, wouldn't want to be wasting it by writing.

Q: Wasting time by writing? Isn't that what you do?

A: No. I love writing so it's never time wasted for me. It's my job.

Q: But you get no recognition for it.

A: Most of the time ghosts don't get recognition. We don't expect our names to be on the book covers, and often we don't go to the launch parties and the book signings but ghostwriters are professional people. We know what to expect. We know that our job is to write for our clients and we are paid for that. The clients get their names on the finished product. A professional ghost would never expect that.

Q: Is it all life stories?

A: No. It can be anything—novels, stories, children's books, articles, blogs, training manuals, poems. I can provide anything the client wants and then fade into the background and allow them to pass the work off as their own.

Q: But won't the client's friends and family know it's not their writing? Surely they'll be able to tell from the writing style?

A: A good ghost can adapt their style so that it sounds as if the work is in their client's words. It's our job to get inside the skin of the client and become them for a short while. If you wanted a tooth filled you'd find a dentist. If you want your car serviced you take it to a garage. You give the work to experts. So if you want something written and don't have the time or maybe the knowledge then it makes sense to hire an expert, a ghostwriter, and let them do it for you.

Points to remember

- There is plenty of ghostwriting work out there.
- Advertising brings in results and gets your name known.
- Networking means finding new friends and new work.
- Stories are everywhere once you train yourself to look for them.
- Newspapers, radio stations and magazines are looking for stories too. You, as a local ghostwriter, could be that story and get yourself publicity at the same time.

3 **Before you begin**

Before meeting your prospective client

Take a few minutes to consider what your prospective client will want to know. This is an email I received from one; short and to the point.

"You said that you had ghosted someone's story. What does this entail and how is payment made/received? How is the time planned?"

Every client wants to know how much the work is going to cost them. They also want to know what the whole process of ghostwriting involves and how much time and effort will be needed from both parties in order to get the job done. They will also be asking how long it will take.

Your prospective client will expect you to know all the answers and be able to give them all the details, after all they are employing you as the expert. Before you leave home for that first meeting you need to have those answers ready.

A major problem when it comes to clients' expectations of their book is that they have been led, mostly by the media, into believing that all writers are rich and everyone gets huge advances. You will need to explain the publishing business to them, gently!

Meeting your prospective client

Once you have contact with a prospective client you need to have an informal meeting to discuss the work and the business arrangements such as deadlines, publisher, contracts, and of course pay. If you contacted them presumably you already know some of their story and you know them, or of them. If they have contacted you and you've not met then that's the first step in the ghosting process.

By far the best way is to arrange a face-to-face chat. This meeting will enable you to discover whether you can get on with the client or not. You are the professional here and it's part of your job to put the client at ease—even if you are nervous yourself—and make them believe you know what you are doing—even if you don't because this is your first time.

- Make sure you are presentable and wearing a welcoming smile.
- Make sure you have pens—in the plural in case one runs out, paper and perhaps a small digital-recorder.
- Make sure you are on time. If you have to make an excuse for being late it will put a dent in the client's confidence in you.
- Make sure you are both certain of the venue.

If you know the subject then you can arrange to meet up anywhere that it is convenient for both of you to do so.

If you have no idea who this person is then stay safe. The meeting place should be on neutral ground for this inaugural session. Meet where there are plenty of other people around. A café would be a good choice.

My experience

A male client called me to ask if I would write an article for him. Naturally I was interested. He then asked if I would go to his house to discuss the work he wanted doing. I said no. He was a total stranger and the idea of meeting there didn't appeal. He then asked if he could come to my house. Once again it was a no, for the same reasons. My suggestion was that we met in town at a favourite café of mine. This is what we did and the gentleman in question turned out to be kind and shy and, in my opinion, very unlikely to be a mass murderer. We sat in a window seat and he ordered coffee and Danish pastries. This was Mistake Number One. It wasn't easy to take down notes with fingers sticky from the Danish pastry. I suggest you don't eat when working. I had also switched on a small voice-recorder so that I would have a complete record of our conversation. This was Mistake Number Two. The background noise of customers chatting, cups and plates rattling and the traffic outside going by almost smothered the voice of my client when, once home, I played the recording back. Do not rely on your voice recorder unless you are somewhere quiet, which you shouldn't be for your first meeting with a stranger.

First impressions

Some experts say that we form our opinions of others during the first ten seconds of seeing them. Others reckon that ten seconds is a generous amount of time and our first impressions are formed in one tenth of a second, and not often changed thereafter. So, if you are the sort of person who trusts their instincts and you feel an instant aversion to your client on meeting them for the first time should you walk away from the job offer? It's not a very professional way of going about things but the decision is yours. No-one else can make it for you. In my experience I have usually been right about clients. If it was dislike at first sight I would walk away, not that that has ever happened. On the other hand if you feel you can put your personal feelings to one side, get on with the work, and feel confident in doing so, go ahead and accept the commission. Remember that you are likely to be spending rather a lot of time in the company of your client so you need to cultivate some rapport. There certainly should be trust between client and writer.

> **Make a note** – If the preliminary chat excites you, or you feel an empathy with your client, then go for it.

> Chriss McCallum advises— *'Check out, as far as you can, that you're likely to get on with your client, and check out their reasons for wanting to write what they want you to help with. Also make sure the project is something you will enjoy doing, otherwise it could become a chore and that will show in the writing.'*
>
> Lynne Barrett-Lee had a lot of anxieties at first about working in collaboration. She says, *'I have a very clear sense of how I want a book to read. I needed to be clear that, as far as was practical, I would have the last word on all matters of style and structure, so we had to have a very frank meeting, in which I somewhat laid down the law about my maintaining creative control!'*

This preliminary meeting gives client and writer a chance to size each other up. Very early on during the meeting you should write down all the contact details of your prospective client:

- Name,
- address,
- phone numbers—home, work and mobile, fax, email.

This first meeting also gives you the opportunity to hear exactly what the client will want you to do. It gives you the chance to draw out the gist, or overview, of their article, speech or story. At this point all you need is the bare bones of the job. You need to know whether this is a project that will interest you. This is not the time to go into the cradle to grave scenario of your client's life, but you do need enough information so that you can make an informed decision. A straightforward speech for the bride's father might sound like a simple commission but if there's some sort of controversy going on between the two families you'd need to know.

> 'I once discovered that a prospective client was involved in an on-going family feud relating to a disputed will,' says Chriss McCallum. 'He wanted me to write his version of how badly he was being done by! I did not feel I wanted to get involved with something like that, so I turned down the job.'

Lynne Barrett-Lee turned down one job at a very early stage.

> 'It was clear we were not going to connect. The client had already written her book, and been trying to find someone to publish it for many years. It was dry as dust to read but a brilliant story and I could see right away how I could bring it to life. The problem became evident right away, however; she really didn't want a) a ghostwriter, as she loved what she'd written, even though she'd had countless rejections and suggestions on how she needed to change it, and b) to bare her soul and talk about her intimate feelings (she'd been through a terrible trauma). Instead, she just wanted to dwell on the facts and her (undoubted) stoicism in the face of them. I did try to explain that it's the human story/the trauma/the emotion people relate to and want to read about, but she was intensely private, and just couldn't do it. A great shame.'

If you are unsure about taking on the job give yourself time to think it over. My advice is never to carry a diary with you. It is then possible to say you will need to consult your diary and see how busy you are. Promise to get back to the prospective client within a certain amount of time. *"I'll let you know tomorrow,"* will suffice. The lack of an available diary is a useful device for those of us who say yes immediately and then regret it later. You could be taking on a huge amount of work and an instant yes or no is not a good idea. Tell the prospective client that you really do need to check to see if you can give them the time they deserve before committing to anything.

Even if you are desperate to break into ghostwriting and keen to get on with your first project you need it to be one that appeals to you, even if only in a small way. Time is precious. Don't waste yours struggling over a project you have no interest in, or one that underpays you. Certainly, if your heart isn't in it, then say no and look for something else that will appeal.

> **Make a note** – If you hold the slightest doubt as to whether you want this job then allow yourself some thinking time. Don't feel pressured into making any hasty decisions.

Getting the facts

It's worth asking, at that first meeting, if there will be anything controversial or upsetting in the client's story. You really need to know as this could sway your decision. As the old adage goes, Forewarned is forearmed.

Learn by my mistake

At our first meeting Pat gave me the outline of her story. She had been a young girl living in a small village in the Welsh Valleys but she had wanted more. After running away and having several adventures, she met and fell in love with a rich powerful man. Her story was to be about their life together. (Mentioned in Chapter 1 under *The shock factor.*) It didn't have a happy end, she warned me. It was a rags-to-riches and back to rags story. I liked Pat, and we are still in contact, but halfway through writing her story a well-known agent got involved and convinced her to tell all. Something I had obviously failed to do! At our next meeting she was withdrawn and I sensed she was uncomfortable about something. It was then that she said, "*I suppose I should tell you about the paedophilia.*"

You can do without surprises like that, especially when you are well into the work. Get the worst bits from your client and then decide.

Keeping your mouth closed

Your moral judgements, politics, religion, any views on life have to be kept to yourself when interviewing clients. You, as a ghostwriter, will have to learn to bite your tongue and keep your opinions to yourself.

"*I do not agree with what you have to say, but I'll defend to the death your right to say it,*" are words from Voltaire, or maybe Oscar Wilde or even Evelyn Hall. They have been attributed to many wise people but, regardless of who came up with them in the first place, they are worth remembering when you are listening to views and opinions you do not agree with.

Think twice about taking on any project if you disagree with the subject's views. These are likely to be expressed over and over in the work they want you to undertake and, as a new ghostwriter, it could prove extremely tough to step back and complete a work on something that is totally opposed to your beliefs. But, if you really think you can be non-judgemental then go ahead and say yes to it. Professionals have learned how to be non-judgemental.

What to lookout for

Certain types of clients should be avoided. If someone is a little bewildered, shall we say, their story might prove to be one huge headache.

Janie Jackson tells the story of her attempt at writing the biography of an ex-Colonel.

'*Our first meeting was a sort of getting-to-know each other chat—though I think the Colonel started on about the ducks even then. The second time I tried to get some order by saying it would be easier for us both if we started at the beginning—where he was born, educated, etc.—but that immediately set him off on the ducks. And I have a vague idea geese were mentioned, too. I seem to remember that at some stage—round about the fourth meeting—he proudly handed me "some notes I've made for you"—dreadful scrawl on exercise book paper—about ducks! Over a period of three months I visited him about six times but never got beyond the way he used to play with the ducks on the farm when he was a kid! What's more—I didn't even get offered a cuppa! With hindsight, I realise that I should have insisted on much more organisation. Given him a definite date to write about, for example. At least some of the situation was obviously due to my own inexperience, I started out on the premise of letting him talk, so that I could jump on the interesting bits and then get more info.'*

There are also clients whose lives, because they are involved in a certain subject like medicine, or mountaineering, will either need to be very clear when explaining things or the job will require a lot of research.

'*I interviewed a retired driver of the famous steam loco Flying Scotsman for Steam Railway magazine. It quickly became apparent that this man had led an extraordinary life, and I considered the option of ghostwriting his life story. We met weekly for some months. It was like peeling off the layers of an onion. Always more to discover, and all of it was interesting. He was very co-operative, and made himself available on a regular basis—an ideal interviewee.*

'*While I was gathering detail, I couldn't help noticing that in retelling particular experiences, he'd recall different things on different occasions. I'd feel I'd covered a topic only to discover a month or two later that some important detail was missing. And in some cases what was missing was simply my lack of expertise in this area. This particular subject area is one where accuracy is essential and there are many people with more expert knowledge than me. So I've come to the conclusion that this isn't a viable project for me.'*

Glynis Scrivens

And what happens if they sound uncertain about the whole thing. Maybe they dither when you mention certain parts of their story and say things like, "*It might be best if we skipped that bit,*" or "*We'll leave that out, shall we?*" There's nothing worse than putting in the effort only to find your client, further down the line changes their mind about the whole venture. If you feel a client doesn't sound entirely sure that they want the work to see the light of day it's wise to give them a no, thank-you.

'My client decided a couple of months into the project that she wanted me to stop pitching her book to publishers and agents. She changed her mind about it being available to the public.'

Julia Anderson

Here's the story of a well-meaning person who thought someone else's life story should be written.

A friend mentioned over coffee that she'd met someone whose stories had to be told. He certainly sounded a fascinating character. For a start, he'd managed to train an ape to be his office assistant. This ape could, on demand, open the combination safe. He could bring requested files. And was generally indispensable. "Tell me more," I said.

She recounted adventures he'd had in his youth. As a school boy he'd sold newspapers on the streets, and regularly had his earnings taken by a policeman. "He has hundreds of stories," she said. "And it should all be written down."

By whom?

Was I prepared to be a ghostwriter for him, as she was suggesting? When I thought it over later, it occurred to me that it was my friend who was pushing the idea rather than the man himself. I hadn't even met him. Alarm bells rang in my mind. I phoned her. "What does he think about this?"

She hesitated then said he had a terminal cancer and had other priorities for his remaining time. She was hoping to persuade him to have his life written up. I had an instant image of being halfway through the project and losing my subject. And what about the inevitable book launches? How could he manage those, assuming he was still alive?

My friend stressed again what a loss it would be if this man were to die with his stories untold. And I agree. But to take on a project like this would be a huge commitment of time and energy for me, AND for him. I've realized he would need to be the driving force for this project to work. And that's what I've had to tell my friend.'

Glynis Scrivens

The person whose story it is going to be needs to be the driving force. If a friend or family member is pushing it then it could be a thankless task trying to get the subject to co-operate.

There are also personalities who demand too much, such as the type who have no opinion on how to go about writing their life story for themselves so allow you to take charge but, when you show them the work, they suddenly develop strong opinions about what they don't want, and that's exactly what you've produced.

There are types who think the job won't take very long. This is because they are not writers and have no idea how much time and effort goes into any sort of writing.

'When I was working eight hours a day on my client's memoirs a friend of his kept asking why it wasn't finished. The comment this friend made about being able to do the work herself in a month or less, undermined the confidence my client had in me. We ended up in a long discussion on the business of writing and writing well. In the middle of it I asked if the "friend" had ever written anything. The answer, naturally, was no.'

Ghost 1

The above also applies for a client who comes along announcing they have an easy job for you. If it's so easy, why aren't they writing it for themselves? "*You might need to do a little research,*" almost certainly means, "*I know next to nothing about the subject and expect you to pad it out for me and fill in all the details.*"

'My client was pretty lazy, hadn't kept any diaries, had a lousy memory and no knowledge of the politics and social conditions of the country he had lived in. As these played a huge part in his story, without him even realising it, there was an awful lot of research for me to do. I found the process demanding but very interesting—and I learned an awful lot about Croatia.'

Ghost 2

Beware of wannabe writers

There are thousands of wannabe writers out there. Some begin to write their own novel, life story or series of children's books and realise that it's not as simple as they first thought. Some will tell you that they could do the job themselves and then give an excuse for not doing so—usually they don't have the time.

The wise ones will ask for help and some may turn up on your doorstep to ask if, as a ghost, you can knock the work into shape for them. As amateurs they will love every word they've written, especially the flowery passages. Remember how you were when you started off? It takes long hours of practise and lots of experience before most new writers learn to edit and polish their work. Many believe that a first draft is the only one necessary. Wannabes can belong to one of two categories. If you're lucky they will want to learn from you. If you're not they will argue over every little change.

Steven had a client who had written tens of thousands of words as notes for his story but asked for it to be ghosted. When Steven began on the writing he explained that all the traumas the client had been through before the actual "real story" began should be spread throughout the book. Several chapters of doom-and-gloom at the beginning would put off any prospective editors, publishers and readers. *"But that's the way it happened,"* the client told him. Steven decided against taking on the job because this client, although a total amateur with no knowledge of the writing profession, wanted the book written his way. He wouldn't listen to any advice from an expert.

'I am always a tad twitchy working with subjects who have serious pretensions towards "being a writer", as both their expectations and acceptance of their own skill-level tend to be a bit difficult to manage and, if they do have sufficient talent, they should be writing the book themselves. Remember, most people you ghost for have no understanding of how publishing works, and have massively unrealistic expectations of how rich and famous their one book is going to make them. (No different to debut novelists in that respect ...) They also often fail to understand that they have little control over jacket design, distribution etc, which can cause friction.

'I've not had difficult clients—I can tell right away if it's going to work, and wouldn't take on a book if I felt there was any tension/friction. Generally, it's more a case of difficult moments. Happily, they are few, but you do need to play go-between between publisher and subject sometimes, which needs huge diplomacy.'

Lynne Barrett-Lee

There are clients who want the work finished yesterday. They demand chapters by such and such a date. They seem fixated by the end deadline—the completion of the manuscript. You obviously reach this, and may even hand in the completed work for their approval several weeks ahead of deadline. Then, while the publisher is waiting, the client ignores the manuscript, consistently puts off reading it and giving approval in spite of your many reminders to do so.

The "*one rule for me and another for you*" types can also be awkward. They are the ones who will take ages to reply to any phone calls or emails about queries you may have but expect an instant response when they ask you questions.

Here's a story to put you off. (It's not mine.)

'I hated ghostwriting. In my experience, you are equal to the client's cook-cum-cleaner! I reckon the so called "author" suffers a sense of guilt (jealousy?) because somebody has to be brought in to do for them something that look so easy on the page. "Hated" because I no longer accept commissions and I am busy writing something which will have my own name on the cover!'

Ghost 3

My experience was the opposite. Ten years on and I am still in touch with Pat, my first subject. We became friends during the writing of her biography and have remained so ever since.

When I asked Zoe King if she had ever had any difficult clients she replied—

'No. They have all been wonderful, and have all understood that I'm a working writer and editor, that I can't necessarily give my entire time to their project'.

And does she have a best experience to share?

'It is very difficult to single out any one experience—the role of ghostwriter is inevitably an interesting one because most of the people who imagine they have a story to tell actually do have. I work only in memoir and biography—I don't ghost fiction.'

Has Zoe ever had to give up on any projects?

'No. Once I've taken on a job, I feel I am committed to it. However, I can imagine that on occasion, there must be personality clashes. So far, I've been lucky.'

Chriss McCallum spoke with her client on the phone to discuss the project, and then arranged to meet him and his partner in a hotel. *'I took my husband along to get his view on them and the story. I felt we should meet because it would have been difficult to work with people I might not like. As it happened, we all got on famously.'*

After the initial meeting

A day or two after that initial meeting with your prospective client you will need to contact them to let them know your decision. Are you going to take on the work, or not? If the answer is yes then there are details to work out and agree on before the work begins.

A few more decisions

Contracts are covered in the following chapter. Do not write a word until you have a water-tight contract between the two of you.

> *'Make sure you have a watertight contract—have it checked out by the Society of Authors before you sign anything. And make sure the terms you are offered are reasonable—there is a lot of work involved.'*
>
> Chriss McCallum

Decide whose name goes on the work. I would not expect anyone to stand up at a wedding, do their speech and then tell the guests that it was written by me. I would not expect any loving husband to add, *"Original words by Lynne Hackles"* to the little verse I'd written for them to copy into the anniversary card they'd bought for their beloved wife. When it comes to the longer work, ghostwriters do not expect their names to be splashed in huge colourful print over the book cover but some are mentioned within the pages.

In Pat's story my name is on the inside page along with the publisher's details because Pat and I shared the ownership of the work.

Zoe King was mentioned in the acknowledgements as "my wonderful editor!" She says, *'Ghostwriters know that the named author gets the glory. At most they might expect a "with Ghostwriter's Name" on the front cover of the books they have worked on.'*

'I told my client that I didn't mind if I was mentioned by name or not. In the end, "As told to and researched by Julia Anderson" was on the inside page of the book.'

Lynne Barrett-Lee shared equal billing as co-writer on the cover of one book. For her next she agreed to it being equal billing, but as "with Lynne Barrett-Lee", as opposed to "and Lynne Barrett-Lee".

'Different people have different feelings about these things,' she says. *'I don't really mind, as long as I share the copyright and the income equitably.'*

One ghost was included in an acknowledgment. It read *"With thanks to x for help with the manuscript."* The ghostwriter, who wishes to remain anonymous, hence the *x*, says, *'He made not one, but two spelling errors in my name, which did not please me one bit.'*

Sharing the workload

There are ways to make your ghosted work simpler. It should not be a chore for either party. There are a few points worth explaining to your client before the work begins.

Meetings

Now is the time to pull out the diary and write in ink the dates and times for joint meetings so that you can discuss the work. Once you have all the information you need from the client you may not need any further meetings. A phone call or email may suffice if you need to ask a few further questions or the client wants to know how work is getting on.

Schedule the meetings to fit in with your writing agenda. If you prefer to write in the morning then arrange to meet your clients after lunch. If you're a night owl and write best late at night, or even in the early hours, then arrange to meet your client during the daytime—perhaps not too early if you've been up half the night working.

Decide how long you are going to work together. This depends on the two of you. If your client quickly tires of reminiscing and turns the conversation to the weather or what they watched on television last night, then schedule short slots. An hour may be too much for some. All day may not be long enough for others. Once again plan your timetable so that it suits both of you.

Julia Anderson recommends—

'Set boundaries when the client can contact you, especially if you are ghosting their autobiography and you become quite matey, after all as their ghostwriter you will probably know more about them than anyone else. My boundaries for being contactable by phone were only during office hours, Monday—Friday. No evening or weekend calls allowed. And if a client called me and it wasn't convenient then a suitable time would be agreed on.'

Involving the client

Ask the client if they have started writing any of the work themselves before you begin. They may have contacted you because their reams of notes became too muddled and panicked them into realising they needed professional help. The more they've written, the less you will need to take down in notes. The client's actual writing gives you a further insight into their personality. You have, in black and white, their vocabulary, their voice.

You can also ask the client to hand over any useful documents. They may have photos, photocopies of newspaper cuttings, certificates, letters …. Anything that is relevant to the work will be helpful and save you time but do keep these papers in a safe place, and do list them and hand your client a copy of the list so that you both know what you have in your care.

Checking your copy

Hand over the work a chapter, or section, at a time, and encourage your client to read it. Explain a little about what sort of feedback you need. Are you on the right lines? Are they happy? Do they want anything changed? Explain that it is easier for changes to be made as you go along, rather than have a whole lot of rewriting to do when you've reached the end. Give them a few tips on reading. Suggest they read it twice. Once for pleasure and then slowly and carefully to check that all names are spelled correctly, dates are right and that all the information they want included in that particular section is there. Seeing their life in print can jog further memories and it's easier to include those as you go along.

Advice

Make sure your client knows that you are the expert and they can ask you for advice or ask any questions they may have about how you are structuring their story. They may not understand why you've changed the order of their story and challenge you. Confrontation isn't necessary if they feel they can ask you questions.

Photographs

If you are going to use photographs in your ghosted book make sure they are the property of the client and get written permission from the client that explicitly says so. Remember that photographs have the same copyright as author's work; that is the copyright lasts until seventy years after the death of the photographer.

If photos are being used then make sure you are paid for your time in dealing with them, or that the client deals with the actual photos. Checking through them, selecting the best, scanning them, tweaking and resizing all takes time. If your client is capable and willing, pass the job onto them. If they aren't capable of doing it then work out a payment for someone else to do the work or for you to do so.

> '*I only charged for writing the book then, somehow, choosing the photos became my job. Where to put them became my job, and resizing was down to me as well. Then when my client wanted them all moved and resized again, it took and cost me more unpaid hours.*'
>
> Julia Anderson

Words of wisdom for aspiring ghostwriters

From Zoe King

'*The first and obvious thing to be aware of is that ghosting won't bring you fame and fortune. It can though offer other, major compensations, not least the knowledge that you have enabled someone who isn't a natural writer to tell their story, and to get it out into the market place to be read. Then of course, however you choose to organise it, there is the income. For the successful ghostwriter, there can be a steady income once you have one or two successful projects under your belt and can advertise yourself a such.*'

From Lynne Barrett-Lee

'*Leave your ego at home! You will not achieve fame and glory with the public (most still do not have a clue who Rebecca Farnworth is, for instance), but if you are professional and good at what you do, you will soon become known — and respected — within the industry. And that's where the work comes from. You also genuinely have to like and be fascinated by people, and be sensitive and non-judgemental in your dealings with them.*'

If you deliver the goods in such a way that the client is completely happy, you'll feel a great sense of relief plus the satisfaction of knowing you've done a good job. That makes both parties happy.

Points to remember

- You can do as much or as little as you like when setting up a ghostwriting business.
- Once you've seen your first client the nerves will start to disappear.
- Those preliminary meetings should be interesting, and fun.
- You are in control. You can say yes or no.
- Some clients will turn into good friends.

4 Contracts and pay

Big dreams

If you've written a novel or children's book, did you ever dream about the future it might have? New writers often dream of agents auctioning their work, six-figure advances, two-book deals, best-sellers, film and television rights. Once we have learned a little more about the business we realise that we can still dream about this scenario but in real life it only happens for a few. It's the same with ghostwriters. Their clients may have extraordinary stories to tell, stories that should be read by millions, turned into films and become box-office successes. It's unlikely to happen but it could!

Coming down to earth

From the other side, the client may have read about the huge payments made to celebrities for their biographies, and be wise enough to know that these were ghostwritten and that the ghost would get a good percentage of the profits. That can put many clients off. They may have a wonderful story but a sickly looking bank balance. You need to advertise your rates as being reasonable so as not to scare away the owners of such stories. But, as one ghostwriter advises, '*Remember you are ghosting because you are a professional wordsmith who enjoys writing, not just because you yearn to see your name on the front cover—so don't sell yourself cheap!*'

Let's say you are approached by a man with a great story. How long will it take you to get enough notes in order to write the book for him? How long will it take you to write up those notes and produce the finished item? Could you do it in a month? Two? How much money would you want to earn in a month? Remember that the average earnings of most freelance writers is around the £20,000 a year mark. That's £400 per week. If you can write quickly and you work full-time at writing, would that money be enough? Take care that you charge enough but do not out price yourself.

Fees

How much should you charge? Now, this is the big question and, unfortunately, there is no set answer. The fee when working for a top celebrity is going to be far more than when working for Mr Jones, down the street. The trick is to match the fee to the client. If you're lucky enough to be asked to ghost for a 'name', someone with huge sales potential, then the fee will be far removed from that of a client who has a great story but has never been heard of.

A ghostwriter has to hand over the credit for writing the work to his client. In exchange the ghost should have the satisfaction of knowing they've done a good job and their client is happy but they also need to feel valued and that's why ghosts expect to be paid a fair whack. Some ghostwriters argue that the fee needs to be high because their name isn't on the product they've created.

Fees need to take into consideration the amount of research that may be required and the length of the work involved.

Ideally the writer needs to be sensible and not overcharge. Walking a tightrope between making a decent income and giving your client a good deal is, well, as difficult as walking a tightrope. On the other hand the client should not expect you to work for nothing. Writers don't really want to starve in garrets, and even garrets these days would have high rents. As writers we need to teach the public that writing is a service like any other. Could you rewire your own house? I doubt it. You'd need an expert. Electricians, plumbers, hairdressers and aromatherapists all get paid for what they do. Can your client write his own book, article, or story? Of course not, that's why he's asking you to do it, and like the aforementioned trades, you are the expert who can supply the service. Therefore you need paying.

You could start off with a fairly low rate in order to attract clients. It can be increased as you become more experienced.

One ghost was offered a down payment before work began, and a decent royalty afterwards. She accepted and later, when offered other work from the same source, realising that the client was a household name, she asked for the down payment to be tripled and an extra 10 per cent to be added on top of the royalties she'd previously been paid. To her surprise, the client said yes.

At the other end of the scale we have one of my experiences. I felt empathy with my client and as she was broke—at one point she had been living in her car—we agreed that I would write for her and get paid once the book was accepted. The split was to be 50/50 but this turned out to be peanuts as all the copies of the book were destroyed a few weeks after publication. At the time it seemed a good idea because she had called a top PR to the glitterati and he'd shown interest in the project. I hadn't ghosted anything as long as a book at that time, but seeing as the project had landed in my lap I felt it was meant to be. Obviously I hoped to make money from it, and further my career.

Sometimes working as I did can pay off. If your client has no money but the possibilities sound good do not automatically refuse the work. Think it over and trust your gut instinct.

Lynne Barrett-Lee says, *'I got, and will continue to work on, a 50/50 split across all income and royalties, with shared copyright. That's the usual deal if a book is taken on speculatively; equal risk and equal reward. Though I am finishing a book right now that I've done for a fee, as the publisher had already bought it, and needed someone to ghost it—but mostly I work on royalties. I'd be happy to work for a fee again, however, if the fee and the book felt right for me. I think it's important to be flexible, because it's also important to make a name for yourself in the industry as a capable, reliable ghosty.'*

Hourly rates

Some ghosts charge by the hour. But how much should one charge? There doesn't appear to be a specified rate for ghostwriting, probably because each job differs and each client has a different sized wallet. Rates for proof-reading and copy-editing vary, in 2011, from £10–£80 per hour. I suspect the busiest proof readers get near to the lower end of that scale.

> *'We agreed an hourly rate and that when/if we were taken on by a publisher we would review the money side.'*
>
> Ghost 4

> *'For that project, I worked at an agreed hourly rate. Later projects have differed, but overall, I prefer at least some upfront or ongoing payment as I may well have to shelve other writing plans in order to focus on the ghosting project.'*
>
> Ghost 5

Lump sums

Other ghosts ask for a lump sum. It can depend on the job and the book's prospects.

> '*I asked for payment in two lump sums—one before I started work, and the rest on completion and the handing over of the work and the copyright. The client originally wanted a shared royalty arrangement, but I wouldn't work like that unless the contract came through a mainstream publisher and I was pretty confident of making enough money to cover my time and work. The contract and payments were all arranged through the agent.*'
>
> Ghost 2

> '*The publishers would not give me royalties despite entreaties by my agent. I accepted a lump sum in the end but did feel that it would have been nice to have had royalties as it was published again after that and also in different languages.*'
>
> Ghost 6

Royalties

If you already have a market for the book and it will be through a mainstream publisher then a down payment followed by royalties may be your best bet. Royalties will keep coming in for a few years, as will Public Lending Rights.

Payment by instalment

If the job is to produce the memoirs of someone who is definitely not in the limelight, and who wants to have a dozen or so copies printed for his family members then a lump sum, or hourly rate is the way to go. Or you could suggest payment by instalments. £x per thousand words, or a cheque after each completed and approved chapter. Payment by instalment is good for both sides of the partnership. The client doesn't have to shell out a huge amount at one time, and the writer gets a steady income.

Chickening out

And what happens if your client decides against committing their secrets to print after you've begun work? There should be a clause in your contract about that possibility.

> *'I have no idea if his story was ever written. I certainly didn't do it but I had spent some considerable time visiting and interviewing him. When we parted company it was amicably and he paid me £400, so it wasn't a dead loss.'*
>
> Janie Jackson

A clause in the contract giving a deadline for the work is a good idea. The deadline works both ways. The writer may be keen to get the job completed and it could be the client who has no sense of urgency.

> *'Everything was progressing so slowly and I had lots of other work on. After several years of being given notes and receiving endless emails there still wasn't enough for me to get to work on and I decided to cut my losses and advised my client to look for another ghostwriter.'*
>
> Ghost 7

Online work

There are companies who advertise online, asking for ghostwriters to produce articles or even books for free. The payment, they say, will be made later. A mention of royalties may be made, or they may even suggest you work for free as you can add the work to your CV, gain valuable experience and build up a body of published work. Beware! If you work for an online company make sure they are trustworthy and get a contract.

Expenses

There will be expenses when ghostwriting, especially when it comes to longer work—books and memoirs, for instance.

Who pays what will need to be sorted out before work begins. The good news is that it's the client who pays.

What expenses are incurred? Actually, anything you use in the course of your work. That means a sum for a certain amount of ink. Inkjets or laser cartridges aren't cheap and you will need to print the work out for your client's approval. Then there's the paper. You may have to post work to your client. List the postage on your expenses sheet. Keep a list of everything. You can always delete items later if you don't think they are fair but you certainly won't remember every postage stamp if you are keeping in contact by snail-mail several times a week or sending out proposals to publishers.

If you have to travel to interview your client then how do you get there? By rail or bus? You need to keep the tickets. By car? You need to log the mileage and charge per mile. Once the client knows that you expect to be paid for any journeys made then they might decide it's easier to get to you. This saves you time and money.

You may need to travel for research reasons, whether it's to a library or museum, or a place of interest in the story. I once drove to a mining village in Wales to see where Pat had spent her childhood. Seeing that steep valley, the long rows of terraced houses and the hills looming on all sides, blocking out sunlight for most of the day, gave me an insight to why she needed to escape. Another trip was made to St Fagan's museum, in Cardiff, where the cinema that Pat's father had managed had been moved to. All this background research helped with my writing.

More on photos

If your client wants to add photographs to their memoir or biography then you could add this time-consuming job on to your expenses. (See chapter 3) However you work it make sure you are paid.

Paying expenses

If your expenses are likely to add up quite quickly to substantial amounts then a 'Pay as you go' agreement would be in order. Otherwise keep a comprehensive list with dates, reasons and costs to pass to the client once the work is complete and achieve a nice lump at the end.

Ghostwriting is a job and you should not be out of pocket at the end of it. Think of it this way—your fee minus inkjets/ laser cartridges, paper, postage, petrol, phone calls, research expenses = not a fat lot, i.e. not much.

Explaining the realities

- Your client will be excited about this project so it is your job to bring them down to earth. Do not allow them to think of best-sellers and Hollywood films.
- If you client self-publishes remind them that there will be lots of selling for them to do.
- Remind your client that there will be lots of selling to do even if a mainstream publisher takes the book. They may get it in the shops but money for advertising will be in short supply, especially for a one-off, which your client's story is likely to be.
- Do not allow your client to contact publishers who are looking for work and advertising in magazines and newspapers. Most will be vanity publishers or will want paying to produce the book.
- Explain to your client that the stories he/she has read in tabloids about six figure advances are in those newspapers because they are such rare occurrences.
- Teach your client how to act when being interviewed. They need to know not to give away too much information and not to order champagne and caviar.
- Stick to set times when you can be contacted.

Contracts

If you and your client are working with a publisher then there is no need for you to draw up a contract. It is you who will be given one.

If you are working without a publishing contract in place then you need to commit something to paper—some rules that you and your client agree on.

If the job is a small one, like a poem, then a written contract isn't necessary. A verbal agreement should be enough. The client asks you to write a poem for her Aunt and Uncle's golden wedding anniversary, you say yes, you write the work, hand it over and get paid.

For longer work, especially books, you do need a contract and if you are already a member of the Society of Authors all you need do is go to their website, www.societyofauthors.org and download their Quick Guide 8—Publishing Contracts. (The Society also has a Quick Guide 15—Ghost-Writing and Collaboration Agreements.) If you are not a member then you can draw up your own contract. It's all about deciding and agreeing on who does what and how you go about it.

When writing your own contract, keep it simple. There really is no need for big words and old fashioned jargon. Leave out the wherewithal, aforementioned, and heretofores. A short letter covering the valid points is enough, as long as you both agree.

Here is one I used when my client had written most of the work himself and needed my help to lick it into shape.

Start off with the date and your names.

Date

CONTRACT between Lynne Hackles and (my client)

I, Lynne Hackles, undertake to proof-read and copy-edit (Title of work), by (client's name).

We agree that I shall receive £x for this work and give all rights in it to (client). My name will not be on, or in, the book.

It is agreed that the work will be sent to me on a memory stick and returned by same, unless arranged otherwise at a later date.

It is agreed that (client's name) will pay £x when sending the memory stick, and the remainder will be paid on delivery of the MS.

Please sign both copies. Return one and keep the other for your records.

This was for a short piece of work which was unlikely to find a publisher.

There are other points to consider and it's wise to cover most if you are doing the bulk of the work.

You might want to add clauses for the following—

- When, where, and at what times you meet and what times you are available for your client to contact you.
- That any tape-recordings, papers, letters, pictures, photos, certificates for use in the work will be handed over to you for a certain amount of time, or until the work is completed.
- That both of you need to agree on any publishing contract you may receive.
- That you will keep quiet about the work and not pass on any information to others until the work is complete (or any other time you agree on).
- Who is responsible for checking the work—you, your client, or both.
- A time limit to find a publisher. Multiple submissions are acceptable now but do you want to be sending the work out for years? Suggest a time span, after which the client can be the one responsible for sending out the work and you can retire from the project.
- Are you going to be writing the proposal if the work is to be sent out to publishers?
- Are you going to be helping with the promotion and selling of the work after publication?
- Who owns the copyright? It can be both or either of you. I have always retained 50% copyright and this includes anything that might happen to the book later, such as film or television deals.
- What the money situation is going to be. Are you going to be paid a lump sum, be paid by instalments or receive a share of the royalties?
- Whether there is a "capping" sum, say anything over £x thousand earned from the book means a change in royalties. You may receive 50 per cent before this sum is reached and then agree to take a lesser cut afterwards.
- Asserting your moral rights. This means that you assert your moral right to be identified as the author.

- A falling out clause in case one or the other of you decide to pull out of the work for reasons of sickness, death, a change of mind, the work has been dragging on for too long—some clients will keep sending you snippets of the work for years so adding a date for when the work can be expected to be completed is a good idea.

You may want to add extra clauses, or disregard some of the above. The main thing is to keep the contract simple and make sure both parties agree on each point. Ask your client if they think there is anything else you need to cover. If you feel happier then consult a solicitor and ask them to draw up a contract for you.

If you are a member of the Society of Authors ask them to check any contract you devise and advise on it.

Libel

When ghostwriting *Sapphire and Sweetboy* Pat and I used a solicitor. This was not so much for the contract but because we needed someone to check this work for libel. Pat's story involved several forms of sexual abuse and she wanted to be sure there was nothing libellous in it.

I trusted Pat and knew from her demeanour that she was telling me the truth but I would not have written huge parts of her story if we had not had proof that what she was telling me was the whole truth. Fortunately she had taped many conversations between her and her husband so we had an account of the major events, in his own voice. These tapes were placed in safe-keeping in case anything should happen but we also ensured that a good solicitor read the manuscript and checked to make sure there was nothing libellous in it. Obviously we had not used names of the people involved.

Libel is when you write anything that makes the person mentioned sound stupid or wicked or anything else that will make others lower their estimation of this person. It is such a difficult subject that, if you have any doubts, it is always wise to consult professional help. Ask a solicitor or The Society of Authors.

Points to remember

- Even big dreams can come true.
- Cultivating your business side is empowering.
- Be confident when discussing fees.
- You know more about the writing business than your client does.
- What you don't know, you can find out through friends or writers' forums and organisations. You are not alone.

5 **Interviewing**

A method to suit—your place or theirs?

You have met your client, agreed to write for them, drawn up and agreed a contract, maybe even started to look for a publisher. Now the real work begins. You need to get all the information for the book and that involves talking to your client and getting the full story from them.

Both client and ghost need to be comfortable with the way the interviews take place, especially the client. If they're uncomfortable then how can you expect to get the best out of them? You will have decided on your meeting place. Ideally it should be comfortable, private and have no distractions. That is easier if the meetings take place in your own home because you can unplug the telephone, make the place warm and welcoming and tell family and friends you will be busy and are not to be interrupted. You will also need to decide when meetings should take place, if at all, and hopefully, by this stage, you will have established some sort of rapport.

> *'Everything looked lovely. My room was clean and tidy. The cushions had been plumped up, there was a jug of water and two glasses on the table in readiness. Talking can make you dry. Also on the table was a large vase of beautiful flowers. My client came in, sat down and immediately began sneezing. She suffered from hay-fever. Ever since then I've made sure there are no flowers around.'*
>
> Ghost 8

If you are going to the client's house then you could suggest a few ideas to them. Tell them that you need to be alone and uninterrupted. Advise them to arrange a time when they are on their own so that you can get down to business.

Some ghosting work can be done via telephone calls and emails but most of the longer work, like books which we are discussing in this chapter, will involve some face to face meetings.

Making a start

If your client has written part of their work themselves, or made lots of notes, then now is hand-over time. It's unlikely that the notes will be useable as they stand but they should give you a start on the story.

> *'The person gave me 60 pages of photocopied hand-written notes—which I typed up to give me the bare bones of their story. The notes were badly written, with grammatical errors and spelling mistakes but that was easy enough to correct. However, as the story stood it was boring. It was a dry list of facts, dates, "and then I did this ... and then I did that." Through conducting telephone interviews, I drew out of her many interesting, funny and poignant stories and I added these into the book. Some interviews I recorded, which then meant I had to transcribe the tapes. That took ages, and some parts of the tapes were inaudible. During some interviews I made notes but couldn't write quickly enough and later had to*

ask my client to go back over things. I did a hell of a lot of research which padded out the book nicely. This gave richness to her stories and brought them alive.'

Julia Anderson

'My client had written about 3,000 words of material, and I tried to incorporate those words, as far as possible, into sections of the text. After that, I would ask her to sit down and write about specific events, as we came to them, and I'd then craft a chapter incorporating her details as appropriate. It was a very organic process.'

Lynne Barrett-Lee

With the client's notes, even if they are badly written or boring, you do have a starting off point. It's possible to write the whole book by using those notes and either emailing or telephoning when problems or questions crop up. On the first reading of the client's writing it's a good idea to list any queries as you reach them. You then have a list of questions for the client the next time you speak.

Zoe King worked in a number of ways—*'I had the beginnings of the manuscript, we talked on the telephone, and also made extensive use of email. I used a small telephone recorder to record our conversations, so that I could refer back to them for accuracy, but I much prefer working by email as that gives me a written record.'*

Recording telephone conversations

If you intend to record any telephone conversations you will need the technology to do so and the client's permission, preferably in writing. In the UK they must know they are being recorded by law. An ordinary digital recorder will not work so you will need to buy the right equipment. Invest in the best telephone taping recorder you can afford and check to make sure it's working before you begin a marathon chat to your client. My recorder stopped after the second sentence because, unbeknown to me, there had been a power cut. They happened on a weekly basis where I lived. It was embarrassing, and sounded a lame excuse, when having to admit this to my client but, thankfully, she was very understanding.

> *'It is worth bearing in mind that the role of ghostwriter can vary. You may write the whole thing from scratch, you may work from notes or diary entries, or you may work more as a "book doctor", working with a manuscript of sorts to produce something publishable. Where you're working at a distance, as I have done on two occasions, the latter is possibly easier in that you have a sound starting point.'*
>
> Zoe King

Taking notes

Some ghosts prefer note taking. And some clients prefer it too. Janie Jackson's client, the Colonel mentioned earlier, was adamant that she didn't use a tape recorder. *'He didn't like them so I had to make copious notes,'* she says. *'Mostly about ducks.'*

Writing down what your client says is fine if you can write quickly or if shorthand is one of your talents, and if you have a good memory. The memory will help when you can't read your own writing or transcribe your shorthand.

I had one client who was fascinated by my shorthand and insisted on standing behind me while I was scribbling away. It was off-putting to begin with but I got used to it and, after a while, he became bored and sat down instead.

The trick when transcribing longhand notes or shorthand is not to leave it for weeks. If you type up your notes soon after they've been made you are more likely to remember what was said and therefore decipher any unintelligible words or squiggles. Many writers, especially journalists, have trained themselves to write quickly. It's part of the job, whereas others barely use a pen and prefer to write directly onto the computer screen—a bit problematic when interviewing a client.

> 'No-one else would be able to read my notes. My partner says my handwriting is worse than a doctor's. That doesn't matter. I can read them and that's all that matters. What I don't tell her is that I occasionally have to rely on memory too and if I left my notes for a week I doubt I'd be able to read them.'
>
> Ghost 9

One huge advantage of note taking is that you, as the ghostwriter, take down only the bits of conversation that are relevant to the work in hand. If you use digital recordings then, when it comes to listening and typing them out, you will have all of the conversation/interview and will find yourself listening to the errs and umms, the silences, the times when the interview went off at a tangent and you had to bring it back on track, and lots of other useless stuff. You will then need to edit as you go.

I have heard of ghosts who charge for the transcribing of tapes. I'm not sure how many clients would agree to that. Surely it's part of the job?

Voice recorders, tea and tissues

Interviews needn't take weeks. A concerted effort on both sides can get the bulk of the note-taking covered in one session but it depends on the client. Some will have more stamina than others.

> 'After we had signed the contract, we met up again for a whole day, when I taped about six hours of conversation. I then worked on writing up the story, using the tapes and my own research.'
>
> Chriss McCallum

An advantage of recording your client's words is that, when you listen back to them, you can hear the pace of their speaking, observe their speech patterns, the tones they use, and their diction. It all helps towards creating their voice when it comes to writing.

Keep plenty of spare backup, say on a pen drive, and batteries. It would be awful to run out of either and have the proceedings come to a halt just when you're getting to the good bits.

Never switch off a recording. One client always gave me the most interesting, personal and gossipy bits when she followed me into the kitchen when I put the kettle on. Some clients may start relating part of their story as soon as they are through the door so be sure to have the digital recorder at the ready. If you have to ask them, once you have set the voice recorder, to repeat what they just said, it won't be the same. The impetus will be gone and the second version won't have the sparkle of the first.

Listening

Listening is one of the greatest talents a ghostwriter can have. It is your job to listen. It is not your job to comment on the morals, life decisions, or exploits of your client. Keep remarks and opinions to yourself. Never interrupt when your client is speaking. Wait until there is a pause, sometimes a rather long one, before asking questions. If you don't speak then clients tend to fill that long pause with further information.

The most important part to interviewing is the listening. Listen carefully. Make sure you understand what is being said. Ask for anything you don't understand to be explained. Try using your own words to repeat what you've been told and see if they agree, or if you've misunderstood, or if they have further information to go into that section. If there's a muddled section or something not quite right play back that part of the recording so that the client can hear their own words and perhaps explain them further.

A client of mine had some terrible secrets to tell. I kept tissues to hand as we were sometimes both in tears. Some of the worst bits were parts she preferred to record when she was alone. The strange thing was that she would whisper these into the recorder just as she would have whispered secrets to a friend.

When you are ghosting for a client with dark secrets never interrupt them when they are in full flow. A question at a time like this can break their train of thought and spoil the mood of confession. Don't interrupt or be tempted to shower them in sympathy if they start to cry. Pass them a tissue and allow them the luxury of telling all. And never, ever, tell them of your own personal experiences. *"Oh, that happened to me, or my friend's daughter,"* is not a professional way of conducting an interview.

> 'My subject and I spent many hours with me asking questions and she answering on to a tape recorder. I felt like her counsellor and at times felt awkward and even downright uncomfortable about listening to some of the intimate details of her life but hey, this was work.'
>
> Ghost 1

Where to begin

Before beginning the interviewing process a ghost can make life easier by discussing the format of the book. For a life story or memoirs, will the client want it written in chronological order? Would that work? For many clients it is easiest to begin at the beginning and work their way through to the end. Chronicling a whole life is such a daunting task that many may not know where they want to start.

As their ghost and mentor you could suggest some chapter titles and then delve into each one to give sub-headings. Here is a very general idea:

- **Before the first memories** – what your subject has been told about being born, given a name and their very early days growing up.
- **First memories** – those the client has.
- **Family** – what is remembered about grandparents, maternal and paternal, aunts, uncles, cousins.
- **And closer family** – parents, siblings.
- **Places** – the houses and towns the client lived in.
- **Upsets and accidents** – traumas such as parents dying or splitting up. Broken arms and tonsillectomies or any other hospital experiences. Sicknesses—measles, mumps etc.
- **School life** – Infants, juniors, senior. Teachers, friends and enemies.

- **Self-confidence** – bullies, being good or poor at school subjects.
- **Out of school life** – games played, days out.
- **Hobbies** – clubs, pets, collections, games.
- **Company** – the good and bad friends and siblings.
- **Transport** – how did they get from A to B? Car, train, bicycle, horse?
- **The lack of things** – having an outside loo, no television, no radiators …
- **Discovering talents** – favourite subjects at school, interests that became passions.
- **Aspirations that came to nothing** – not learning to play the piano, discovering that you were too short and plump to be a ballet dancer.
- **Dreams** – and how they came to fruition.
- **Careers**
- **Crises** – major dramas or setbacks.
- **Love** – first love, last love, doomed love, everlasting love, betrayed love.
- **Children** – having your own, seeing them grow.

The above, to mix metaphors, barely scratches the iceberg. Depending on your client's story you will be able to come up with the right chapter and sub-headings. You won't use sub-headings in a life story but they can be useful in keeping the story on track.

Other clients' stories may be about one stage of their life so the above chapter listing suggestions wouldn't apply.

Interviewing techniques

Some clients won't need much interviewing. They will be happy to talk their life through with you and your purpose will be to ask questions if you need further information on any points.

'An elderly client was obviously lonely. She had outlived all of her contemporaries and was living alone. As soon as I went in through her door she would regale me with

> stories. I don't think I had to ask a single question. Her life simply poured out of her.'
>
> Ghost 10

> 'I think every commission is different. Some older celebrities enjoy sitting chatting to their writer.'
>
> Ghost 3

> 'In my last book, my subject would agonise over every word, whereas with this one, they just let me write what I like. They are particularly happy to let me stage scenes and invent dialogue. As long as it's true to the spirit and the facts, that's just fine by me!'
>
> Lynne Barrett-Lee

Others will need prompting or even interrogating, in the gentlest way, of course. It's a ghostwriter's job to draw out all the details of the subject's life. You will have to ask personal questions about them, pry into the corners of their lives, and show no disapproval or horror when they reply. You need to be willing to ask the pertinent questions and dig a little deeper in order to get the right material and write a good book.

Listen carefully and read between the lines. If you are recording the interview then keep a note book handy to jot down any questions you need to ask later. Don't allow a client to gloss over the details. They may start talking about a certain aspect and give very little information. For example they may say something like, *"After my father left us,"* and then carry on with how life was. Your job is to find out why the father left and what affect it had on your subject, her mother and any siblings.

Ghosts don't show disapproval or disgust but what they should show is their ignorance. If your subject starts talking about something you know nothing about then admit that to them so that you can get all the information you need in order to understand. Of course you can research later so that you will have more in depth knowledge but if you haven't a clue what glycolysis means when the word crops up, ask.

Questions

Never ask questions which can be answered with a yes or no. These are called closed questions. The person being interviewed can, and often will, give a one word reply, unless they're a politician. You'll never manage to ghost a whole book if all your questions are answered with a yes or no. Questions beginning with what, where, when, how, why and who will get replies of more than one word. The ones that are answered with a yes or no tend to begin with phrases like Do you, Did you, Have you?

Examples

Closed question – Did you think he was telling you the truth?

No.

Open question – What did you think he was telling you?

Certainly not the truth. It was all lies. I knew what he'd been up to …

Followed by another open question – And what was that?

Closed question – Did you feel upset?

Yes.

Open question – How did you feel?

I was mad. I could have murdered him on the spot. My heart was thumping …

If you know that you are going to discuss a certain subject or era in the interviewee's life then you can prepare a few questions beforehand.

It's no use asking a shy client to *"talk about themselves for a bit"*. This is a phrase I've heard used more than once at the beginning of a television interview. Your shy client will need prompting and encouraging. When they begin to talk do not interrupt with other questions. Allow them to finish what they are saying and encourage them with an occasional nod or a single word so that they know you are listening. '*Yes*' is good, or *"really?"* when they tell you something interesting and will be expecting you to respond.

'*Tell me what happened?"* isn't good either but if the client has given you part of an experience you can prompt them with "And what happened next?" "What did you do/say/think?"

You will gradually learn when to speak and when not to. It's worth waiting a while when the subject has answered your question as there may be more information to come. Don't forget to leave that short pause after they appear to have finished. Often they will feel obliged to fill it and that's when you get the added details.

Not enough material

If you don't have enough material perhaps you are still not asking the right questions. Be nosier. Explore other avenues. Don't forget the little things that make a story real—their favourite foods, toys, clothes, music …

Recap

If you reach a point where you are stumped and don't know what to ask next, you can recap. Go over what the client has said. Sum up what they have just told you and that may prompt them to add further details. At the same time it will give you a chance to collect your thoughts together and decide where you need to go next.

Look and listen

Keep your eyes on your client. Stop asking awkward questions if they begin to fidget or look uncomfortable. If they look as if they are flagging then take a break. Make coffee. Show them around the garden. Give them a chance to relax, recuperate, and then continue.

By watching your client you will see which bits of their lives made them happy and which times were unpleasant.

You will see when they need to change the subject—you can always go back to that place at a later date.

If your client looks down discreetly at his wrist watch you know it is time to stop, even if you are nowhere near the agreed time limit. Some sessions will be harder than others and there will be times when very little is achieved. There will also be those times when a huge amount gets done.

Body language

When interviewing face to face you are able to judge facial expressions and look out for body language. Looking down to the left means your client could be lying, and would you trust them if they couldn't look you in the eyes when answering certain questions?

Some body language is easy to decipher. A smile says I'm happy. One of those wonderful Gallic shrugs says I don't know. Gestures like shrugging, a person's posture and their facial expressions can say a lot but remember that body language works both ways. While you are watching your client they are also watching you. Your client yawns and you think they are tired or bored. You yawn and know that you need a break, some fresh air or just need to open a window. Explain or they may think they are boring you, and you don't want that.

A person tilting their head to one side could show that they are bored, or the tilting could be a habit they have. Unless you are an expert don't automatically assume that your reading of the client's body language is right. If they touch their face while answering a question it could be because they are keeping back some information, not telling you the whole truth, or if may be that their face is sore or itching.

You avert your eyes, tug at the lobe of your ear or rub your chin. All of these actions may mean nothing or they could be signs that you do not believe what you are being told.

Take note of your client's posture. Sagging is easy to read. The posture sags and so does everything else.

Carrying on

After seeing your client at the initial meeting it is possible to work via phone calls and email. Personally, I would need to see the person at least once. Without that I wouldn't have a picture of them in my head. How can you write someone's life story when you haven't a clue what they look like or how they act? If they are a celebrity you will only have seen the persona they portray when in the limelight which might be an act, completely at odds with the real person.

An upside to telephone interviews is that, as the ghost, you get plenty of time to decide on your questions before speaking to your client. The same goes for email. Email is an easy method if you are interviewing another writer because their answers will be well written but you are unlikely to ever ghost for a writer. They can produce their own work. Email isn't so simple when your interviewee is the one who would needs a ghostwriter to tell his/her life story. You will have to word questions very carefully in order to get the answers you want and you may have to send several emails in order to clarify the answers you receive.

Points to remember

- Your client is probably more nervous than you are.
- Ghostwriters hear amazing stories.
- Listening is a great talent. The good news is that it can be learned.

6 The actual writing—life stories

One-minute overview

In this chapter
- Collating the notes
- Getting into character
- Research
- Using their voice
- First memories
- Opening paragraphs
- Prologues
- Chapter by chapter

Collating the notes

You have finished interviewing your client and have reams of notes or a collection of voice recordings. What happens next?

Every writer will find their own way of working and what works this time may not work the next. When we had been recording Pat's story she didn't give me information in any sort of order. Being new to ghosting I didn't have the experience, or sense, to keep her going in a chronological order which would have made life easier for me. She hopped from decade to decade because one memory would lead her to another. She might recall playing with a friend when she was still at Junior School and that would lead to who the friend married and what sort of life she led and how Pat played her part in it.

My solution was to type up all the recordings, print the whole lot out and then read through, cutting up sections with scissors and dropping them into chapter piles. I started one for the very early days, one for school, one for jobs and so it went on until everything was in chronological order.

At the same time I was highlighting aspects that were the most important. This process took time but, once done, it became much easier for me to work with.

If you are lucky and your client told their story in chronological order then you could type out the tapes or listen to them a bit at a time, and using what you hear, write up your story.

Getting into character

Not all clients can be likeable but remember they are all clients and they are paying you to do a job. It's not compulsory to like them and you certainly don't have to become lifelong friends though that's not unheard of.

What you do need is to know your subject well enough to be them. You will need to get into character before you begin writing their story. You need to step into their shoes so that you can see and feel life as they do. If you write fiction you'll know how to get into a character. Sit quietly for a while and imagine being them. Like a method actor, think yourself into their life. Imagine one of the scenes they have told you about. Put yourself into their position and try to understand how and why they reacted as they did. If your client talks about a bereavement and can only tell you that they were devastated then it is up to you, as the ghostwriter, to put devastated into words that will paint a picture and allow the reader to share in the emotions. You could do this by calling upon your own feelings at being bereaved.

Emotions

You know how it feels to be angry, sad, in love ... Your client knows too but he or she may not be able to put their feelings into words. That's your job. Whenever possible use the emotions you've experienced and transplant them onto your client. If they have experienced something you never have then the writing of that will be up to your imagination but ask lots of questions first. Your client could be holding back because something in their past is still too painful to talk about.

'I remembered how my own grandmother had died. She had been a great influence on my life, just as my client's mother had been. I remembered how my entire world was suddenly changed, that there was a huge empty gap where my grandmother had always been. I could not imagine my life without her being in it. I transferred my emotions to my client and when she read them she cried and told me that was exactly how she felt.'

Ghost 8

Similarities

The easiest autobiography to ghost has to be one that is similar to your own life. For instance, if you both grew up in the same location, were educated at the same sort of schools, held the same beliefs, had the same ambitions, then you have a head start. Your life doesn't need to be a carbon copy of theirs but if you can find one or two places, hobbies, interests, people, anything you share it's got to be helpful. Even losing someone close, as above.

Example

I knew what Pat had been through at school. She didn't refer to it as bullying but as *"being different"*. That was because she wore a calliper on her leg and couldn't join in sports and the general running around the playground that the other children did. She was sometimes called names. I could relate to that as I had bad facial scarring and my name at junior school was Scarface. I was sure I knew how Pat felt when she was called names but, as a ghostwriter, I knew her experience, though similar to mine, would also have differences so I listened carefully when she explained her feelings.

More of a challenge

It's more of a challenge when you have to ghost for someone whose life couldn't be further removed from your own.

You also have to listen carefully to these clients, draw out all their emotions and thoughts.

If you have only ever burned yourself with a hot pan and suffered a blister then you will not only need endless information from a client who has been in a terrible house fire and suffered 40 per cent burns but will also have to draw on your own imagination. Relying solely on the notes and interview tapes from your client will not be enough. You will definitely have to use some imagination so that you can step into their shoes, and you will need to do some research to get more background information about certain aspects.

Research

If your client has an injury or illness you may need to do some research. For the above story you might need to visit a burns unit, research the treatment of burns and the follow-up surgery. The client's explanations may not be enough. You, as the ghostwriter, need to fully understand what you are writing about.

Visiting locations

Having some time out to visit locations might help you understand more about your client. If you have only ever lived in a large detached house and your client came from a long row of terraced houses, a walk along such a street would give you a feeling for it. You would understand more. Getting inside such a house would be even better.

Visiting the Welsh valley that Pat grew up in gave me the sense of claustrophobia she had experienced. She had always wanted to escape and, once there, I could see why. She had told me of her longing to see the world and experience the bright lights. Nothing could have been farther removed from her dreams than that valley with the high mountains on either side, blocking out the sun, and the rows of tiny terraced cottages built into the mountainsides.

To visit locations, with or without your client, would be worthwhile. If your client accompanies you to a few places that meant a lot to them and were important to the book they would no doubt expand on their experiences and emotions as they showed you around their old haunts. These places would jog their memories and they might come out with more material for you. If you are alone then you can submerge yourself in the place without interruptions. Just list any questions as they come to you so that you can ask the client later.

Checking facts

When it comes to facts you will need to check them or ask your client to do that for you. If a client is talking about Coronation Day and gives a date for it then make sure that date is right. The Coronation of Queen Elizabeth II was on 2nd June 1953. Do not assume that your client will give you the correct information. For instance, if they are in their sixties and reminisce about their father buying them chocolate buttons as a treat on the day of the Coronation then they are wrong. Cadbury didn't market chocolate buttons until 1960.

If you include something that isn't correct someone is bound to put you right once the book is in print and you nor your client will want that to happen. If you check your facts online than make sure you use several sources to verify each query, and that they are reliable ones.

Memory

There is a well-known song from the film, *Gigi*, called *I Remember It Well*. It is a duet where the two reminisce about their first date and disagree over every memory. If your view of a shared situation differs from that of your client don't argue. They remember it differently, that's all. Facts are facts and cannot be changed but memory is fickle. It's not foolproof and though your client may swear that certain things happened exactly as they've told you, other people concerned may have a completely different take on events. If your client mentions that he and his sister disagree on, for example, how their father was bankrupted it would pay you to add a disclaimer at the beginning of the book. "The memories in this narrative are as I, Jane Smith, remember them."

Using their voice

Writers are told to find their own voice but ghostwriters need to find many voices—those of their clients. This can, at times, be a challenge.

It is important to have not only enough information but enough insight into your subject so that you can write in their voice. During the interviews, if you have had face to face ones, then you will have learned a lot more than you could during telephone conversations or from tapes. You will see how your client behaves, notice their body language, see if they smile often, lose their temper … You have time to make up your mind about how genuine they are.

Your task is to use their words whenever possible, and when it's not possible you have to put your words into their mouth but they still need to sound like your client might have said them.

Love is a drug is an expression I have never used. It is one that a client came out with and I underlined in my notes, knowing I wanted to use it in their story. You should do the same if your client comes out with an expression that you like, or one that surprises you. Make sure you use the good stuff they give you.

Clever words

I often tell writing students to write how they speak, but some can't. They insist on using a more literary style and tell me how a character in one of their stories purchased an ice-cream. What's wrong with buy? And how about traversing down the street? Have you ever traversed to the bus stop? No, I didn't think so. We walk. A few novice writers believe they need to use clever words but it's not true. If you try to be too clever it often doesn't work. But, saying that, you do need to speak in your client's voice so if they actually did say traversed and it came quite naturally to them, would you use it? The answer is yes if that's not the only unusual quirk in their speaking. If their language is a little dated you need to get that over in the writing.

> 'One client who had missed out on an education had a limited vocabulary but had picked up some magnificent words. In amongst all the monosyllables he'd throw in belligerent, nauseating, paraphernalia, eschew and laudable. He evidently knew the correct meanings and used them in appropriate places so I kept them in the writing because they were him.'
>
> Ghost 10

Dialect

If English isn't the first language of your client then you need to capture their speech pattern in your writing. Don't try to write dialect throughout, it's too exhausting for the reader. Use phrases the client uses, get the flow of their speech and the rhythm of their words.

This scene took place in a Welsh working men's club.

> John was struggling to get between the closely packed tables. In the dim light and with a tray loaded with drinks he stumbled and beer got spilled all over this girl's dress. The girl shouted but he took no notice and carried on even when her boyfriend got up and said, 'Oy, just a minute, Butt. Look what you've done. Ain't you going to say sorry?'
>
> If John had had any sense he would have apologised but he was short on sense and answered, 'Bugger off.'
>
> The boyfriend made a grab at him.

I wrote the scene almost as my client described it. Naturally it needed tidying up and editing but I used her words as closely as possible. My client had said the beer had been spilled all over *this* girl's dress. It was the way she spoke.

And when it came to the dialogue I didn't attempt to give every word a Welsh twist but the Welshness came across in *Butt,* a common word used in South Wales with the same meaning as mate or chum.

Inventing dialogue

Is it allowed? Yes, you can put words into people's mouths. Your client may tell you of some conversations, as above, but no-one can be expected to remember the exact words that were said ten, twenty, fifty years ago, or even this morning.

Make the dialogue sound realistic and fit the character who is speaking. Make sure it doesn't ramble. Remember dialogue should let the reader know more about the character who is speaking, or it should carry the story forward.

In some cases you will need to take care over using direct speech. e.g., *'I've been into town and picked up a prostitute,'* he said.

If it involves anything which might be classed as libel or if someone is admitting to something illegal then, even if it's true, it's wiser to use indirect speech. e.g., He said that he had been into town and picked up a prostitute.

Swearing

I kept the swearing in the scene at the working men's club because it was real. No use being prudish when it comes to describing a fight scene in a club. There's going to be swearing. Without it the scene would have been unbelievable. (It got worse later.)

My client was fond of bugger and it featured often in her conversation. If she ever needed to swear out came bugger. She was short on other expletives.

Clichés

I know a man who peppers his conversation with clichés. *"You've hit the nail on the head,"* he says. That's soon followed up by, *"You could have knocked me down with a feather,"* or

"*You're making a mountain out of a molehill*". I find myself holding my breath waiting for the next one.

If I had to ghostwrite this man's autobiography I would use some of his clichés but certainly not as often as he does.

Have you noticed—you must have—how many times certain phrases are rolled out by ordinary folk and celebrities alike? If they are asked how they feel they exclaim *devastated*, or if it's good they *are over the moon*. Another word which crops up far too often is *basically*. And how about *you know what I mean*? I am sure you can add to the list and probably, like me, you wince when these clichés constantly crop up.

As an example let's take a footballer. You are writing his biography. When you discuss him losing an important match he says, '*Basically, I was devastated.*' When talking about one he won one he says, '*I was over the moon, you know what I mean?*' This is the way he speaks and you could use all of those phrases once or twice but use them as many times as he does and you'll lose the reader too. These dire phrases look worse in print and become far more noticeable.

When it comes to describing emotions many people will be stumped and roll out these clichés. As a ghostwriter you need to put your client's emotions into words. It's why they are employing you. They cannot do it for themselves. This may mean using their favourite clichés every so often but, if you describe a scene for them, in your words, it can bring them to tears, or make them laugh and they will tell you, "*That's exactly how I felt*".

First memories

Biographies so often begin with the author's first memory, or an account of the day of the birth. Both are natural starting off points but you will need to find a new way of saying, "*I was born on 6th February ...*"

For a twist on the beginning of a life take a look at Charles Dickens' opening chapter of David Copperfield.

To begin my life with the beginning of my life, I record that I was born ...

And most of us remember that it was as the clock struck midnight that David arrived in the world.

'It was remarked that the clock began to strike, and I began to cry, simultaneously.'

If a ghostwriter can come up with an original beginning to the beginning and catch a reader on the opening page, they've done a good job. But not all subjects have exciting births, baby years and childhoods. Their main story is what, as adults, they become or have to undergo, though the childhood always gives an indication as to how the character of the subject develops.

Opening paragraphs

We know that the first page has to grab the reader's attention so that they will want to buy the book and carry on reading. Beginning with "I was born on 4th July in a little town called …" isn't going to do that.

Lynne Barrett-Lee began her book with a short piece about the aftermath of an accident. The book, *Never Say Die*, is the story of a paraplegic. At fifteen years of age Melanie Davies was paralysed from the chest down when she was knocked off a motorbike. Here is the opening to her story.

Never Say Die

… I don't know how long it was before I fully woke up, but when I did, everything felt different. My eyes opened and for a moment it seemed that I must have been hit on the head. There was no pain at all, but a face loomed above me. A manly face. Rugged. Unfamiliar. Concerned. I wanted him to save me, but straight away I noticed that there was worry in his expression and sadness in his eyes. He asked me a question, but I didn't really hear it. I felt terrified. Why was he looking at me that way? Then he asked me again, and this time I did hear. "Can you," he asked, "move your feet for me, sweetheart?" I had no choice but to answer with a question of my own, because I didn't understand what was happening. Where were they? Where were my feet and my legs? Where was the rest of my body? …

Sapphire and Sweetboy

One of my clients, Pat, had a challenging childhood. We added a prologue to her book to give a taste of what was to come. This was because her life was in two completely separate parts. The prologue was from the time she was living in luxury and married to a multi-millionaire. But the story began when her only home was a tent on waste ground. Chapter one begins;

> *My very first memories are of playing in the dirt, arranging stones into pretty patterns and pulling up tufts of grass, outside our tent.*

I was hoping that the mention of the tent would draw the reader into the story.

> *Jenny, my sister, younger than me by fifteen months, was in her pram. At night the pram would be left outside, turned upside down so it wouldn't get wet if it rained. I felt sorry for the pram being outside while we were all snuggled up together—Mum, Dan, Jenny and me, all curled up, nice and cosy inside our tent.*
>
> *The tent was our only home for a while. Dad had lost all his money in a bad business deal.*

So, my subject had a very bad start to life but was to claw her way up, marry a very rich man, be married in a cathedral and receive invitations to the Queen's garden parties. Her story was like a Catherine Cookson saga, but without the happy ending. As if being a toddler living in such conditions, we had more traumas to throw into this real life plot.

And it gets worse …

As a baby I had been slow to crawl and standing up was difficult for me. Then I was taken ill and afterwards couldn't walk at all. There had been an outbreak of polio at about this time and the doctors were divided in their opinion. Some diagnosed me as having contracted polio, others believed my problem was a birth defect.

If this had been fiction the author would have used devices like these in order to get the reader to feel sympathy and begin to be attracted to the main character. There is no reason why you cannot use the same devices as used in fiction to draw in your reader and get them wanting to know what happens next.

In fiction the main character has problems which they have to overcome, by their own means. This is what endears the character to us. If anyone else provides the solution to the problem then we feel let down. Whether the story is fiction or true life we want to read about feisty characters who decide what they want out of life and set out to achieve just that.

Avoiding chunks

Pat had physical problems which she overcame through bravery. We made sure these problems were not given all in one huge chunk but slipped in throughout the early chapters covering Pat's childhood. We did not want to write a misery memoir.

The ovarian cyst had hidden the fact of my mother's pregnancy and the pressure of it might have been what affected the whole of my left side. No-one has ever been sure. All I know is that my left hand is no good for gripping things with and I have always walked with a limp.

And later,
From the age of four a calliper supported my left leg. It accompanied me until I was twelve years old.

If your subject had lots of problems growing up do not go on relentlessly listing them. Use them sparingly throughout the narrative. Readers do not want to be bombarded with endless gloom. Yes, you are writing true-life but you need to do it in a way that makes it interesting, and not off-putting, to the reader.

Prologues

Pat and I decided to add a prologue to her biography. The biggest events of her life happened after her second marriage. The early upbringing was the opposite but gave the background to her story and showed that she was a feisty character who was determined to succeed. Her first husband was a bus conductor with a violent temper. The second was a multi-millionaire with a secret. I suggested we make the prologue short and use it to hint at the secret this second marriage held. This would be another way, besides the first memories of the living in poverty in a tent on waste ground, to get the reader wanting to know the full story.

Here is the prologue we used.

I can see it all now, in slow motion.

My husband was lying across the bed. He looked up when he heard me. Tears were streaming down his face.

'James, whatever's the matter?' I cried. 'What's happened?'

In a split second so many awful things crossed my mind. He'd had an accident in the car, killed someone. Lost his job. One of his family had died.

As I ran to him and cradled him in my arms I was prepared for the worst. Whatever had happened I would be there for him. Nothing could be that bad that we couldn't cope with it together. How wrong I was!

'Tell me,' I coaxed him.

And through his tears I heard words I didn't understand. Something about a Sweetboy and a big row. Sweetboy didn't love him anymore.

'My God,' I cried, as realisation dawned. No, I'd got it wrong. It couldn't be. 'What are you talking about?' I couldn't believe what my brain was telling me. 'My God, who the hell is Sweetboy?'

And then he told me.

But we didn't tell the reader. They had to buy the book and read on to find out.

Page turners

A good read is often called a page turner. These are written by good story-tellers who know how to keep a reader turning page after page because they need to know what happens next. There's no reason why a life story, especially one where your client has had to go through terrible ordeals, shouldn't be a page turner. The secret is in the pace of the story and the chapter endings. End a chapter on a high note or a cliff-hanger so the reader will want to carry on.

Example

The following is the end of Chapter One from *Never Say Die* by Melanie Davies and Lynne Barrett-Lee.

> *The only warmth was in my mouth, but then also in my heart, as Juli's face suddenly appeared. For a moment I felt calmer. She was here. She would help me. But she was crying and telling me to try not to move and saying sorry and holding onto my hand. I tried to tell her it wasn't her fault but when I spoke a red mist sprayed all over my visor. Now everybody seemed to be shouting at once. 'Internal bleeding!'. 'What's happening?' 'Where's the ambulance got to?' But almost immediately I realised what had happened. I'd bitten the tip off my tongue, and the warmth in my mouth was my blood.*
>
> *I was grateful when the blackness claimed me this time and so, evidently, was my body, because I must have been unconscious for some time. When I next came to it was to the sound of approaching sirens. That was all I could hear now. No other sound at all. I'd retreated into a safe house somewhere in my brain, shutting the door on the horror. I knew I wouldn't be able to keep it out for long, but I chose to remain there, hiding, and praying. Our Father, I chanted desperately in my head, who art in Heaven …*

Who wouldn't want to read on and discover what happened next?

Miss out the mundane

Miss out the mundane or keep it to a minimum. An account of someone's life doesn't need every little action in it. This is the mistake some amateur writers make. They want to include absolutely everything and it doesn't work. Some parts will need glossing over and others will need to be made the most of. Your client may not realise which is which. They may want most of the book about their childhood yet the glowing jewel in their story is the day they were kidnapped at the age of 21 and how they were rescued. How that affected their life afterwards is also important but the leading up to it needs to be kept short and to the point. Obviously there would be a reason for this girl to be kidnapped so if she was from a rich family they will need to be a part of the story but the book is not really about them. It's about the kidnap and aftermath. Keep the main point main.

Chapter-by-chapter

Not all ghosts may agree but I found it easier to hand over each completed chapter as it was written. I wanted to know that I was working on the right lines and that my client was happy with the way her story was being told. Handing it over to the client for approval can be scary. What if they don't approve, don't like it, want changes made? All these things are easier to cope with if only one chapter has been written and not an entire book. Ask your client to read the chapter, making any comments in the margins or between the lines—this is what wide margins and double spacing are all about—and then get them to sign it. That way there can't be any arguments at the end.

The end

When your client has read and approved that final chapter you need to go back to the beginning. This is when the process of editing, polishing and proofing takes place. Work your way slowly and carefully through the whole book, editing, tweaking, making every sentence as good as it can be before it's ready to go out into the world.

Points to remember

- Writing and researching can be enjoyable.
- A group of six people will all have different memories of the same party.
- Draw on your own emotions and transfer them to your client's story.
- Don't think about the whole book. Take a chapter at a time.
- Don't think about a whole chapter. Take a scene at a time.

7 Non-fiction books and articles

One-minute overview

- What is non-fiction?
- Where to find clients
- Subjects you can cover
- Interviewing

What is non-fiction?

Non-fiction? Surely life stories are non-fiction? Yes, but in a library those will be found under biographies and autobiographies. There are so many other types of non-fiction that are available to ghostwriters. If you want to know about any sort of subject it will be listed under non-fiction. There is a far greater market for non-fiction and therefore far more openings for it.

You may never have considered writing a non-fiction book because you do not know enough about any particular subject. You may not, but others do and very often those that do either can't write, don't have the time to do so, or the thought of writing about their specialised subject has never occurred to them. They may have the knowledge but not the ability to write about it. And that's when a ghostwriter steps in. You have the advantage of being able to put words onto paper or screen and you can do it for them.

Where to find clients

The clients are out there. It is up to you to find them or give them every chance of finding you.

- Keep your eyes and ears open for subjects and people who sound interesting and approach them with the idea of you ghostwriting for them.

- Lookout for interesting talks and presentations to go to. The speaker may be good at speaking but unable to write down what they know.
- Add to your advertisements and promotional material the fact that you are willing to ghostwrite specialist subjects.

One ghostwriting job can lead to another and one satisfied client will recommend you to their friends and your business will grow.

You can advertise that you are prepared to take on any type of ghostwriting work, or you can become even more pro-active and listen out for these enthusiastic people. You will be looking for those who are passionate about their subject, their hobby, job, collection …

In every town there are experts on local history. Most have produced books or booklets but there may be some experts who talk about the history to friends, have studied it but aren't able to write it for themselves.

If you hear a person discussing their collection of old postcards and they sound enthused ask them if they've ever written about them. They may have always wanted to but not have the ability, or they may never have given it a thought and be delighted when you suggest it's something you could do for them.

Listen out at parties, bus-stops, meetings. Read the local newspaper. You are looking for people discussing their hobbies, the sport they are involved in, the collections they have, the work they do, the charity they have set up … in fact anything where they actually sound as though they love what they are doing. If you can get their love of the subject across in words then you'll make a perfect ghostwriter for them.

Subjects you can cover

The answer to that is practically everything. You may need to do extra research when writing non-fiction books and you need to be sure that the information your client is giving you is correct. Many writers love researching facts and figures.

Others prefer not to. If you are one of the former then ghostwriting non-fiction could be right up your street.

Keeping, caring, collecting, doing, making

People keep cats, dogs, snakes, bees and all sorts of other animals and insects. They may run a small private zoo or have started up a home for strays and unwanted pets. These are the sort of people who will be passionate about what they keep, and why, and they will want to encourage others to feel the same. What better way than through a book, or at least some articles for magazines?

People care for elderly and/or sick relatives. They may have plenty of good advice to pass on to others. They may care for elderly vehicles, painstakingly restoring them, and they will certainly be knowledgeable and passionate about their cars, bicycles, tractors, whatever …

Whatever item you can think of someone, somewhere, collects it. From varieties of apple trees to xylophones, they'll be out there somewhere and you might bump into one of them, or get to hear about a collection, and think, "*I could write about that*".

They hang-glide, bungee-jump, climb mountains, dance, attempt to skip for longer than anyone else in the world, make the longest sausage, knit the longest scarf, run the smallest theatre … If they love their hobby they might want their opinions and experiences written down.

The general public get up to all sorts of things and have weird and wonderful hobbies. They make cakes for all occasions, knit coats, design retro-style dresses, make candles, draw cartoons for visitors to garden fetes. You name it someone does it and the more obscure it is the more interesting it could turn out to be when written about.

Hobbies, businesses, beliefs

For many, hobbies turn into businesses and a proprietor may want to celebrate ten years of his business by producing a little book, or a hundred years with a bigger one.

I was asked if I would consider ghostwriting the history of a restaurant. The business was coming up to its 25th anniversary and the owner wanted a pictorial record of those years, right from when he turned a barn into an eating establishment.

> 'A friend had started a Mind, Body, Spirit type of book but was struggling. He asked me for help. "It all sounds so flat and uninteresting," he told me. When this man spoke he was able to enthuse those listening but he was unable to do the same thing when the words were written down. Through ghostwriting I did that for him.'
>
> Ghost 7

How to

The public want to know how to lose weight, look younger, get fitter, run a business, set up a bed-and-breakfast, show their pets, cope with computers, research their family tree and a million other things. There are people out there who know how to do all of these things, plus others we've never even dreamed of and they may have dreamed of writing a book aiming to share their knowledge. You could do that for them.

Training manuals

There are teachers and speakers who are good at what they do but cannot put what they do onto paper. When they are in front of a class or audience they are gifted at getting their information across but if they had to write it down so that the audience could buy their words to take home and reflect upon, they couldn't do it. You could! You could offer to write up their speeches, lessons, notes. These could turn into training manuals or even books, depending on the subject matter and length.

Interviewing

When writing for non-fiction markets and on specialised subjects make sure your client gives you the facts. Check them through with him; ask for more detail if you think you need it.

Often when someone knows a subject inside out they will leave out important details. This is because the subject is so close and familiar to them that they forget the little things they need to include so that others will understand it.

Keep asking those six important questions—what, where, when, how, why and who. Make sure you understand what you are being told. If you don't understand a certain point then how can you write it so that the reader will understand?

Points to remember

- Non-fiction is easier to sell than fiction.
- There is a huge market for works of non-fiction.
- The public have interesting hobbies, pastimes and interests that you could ghostwrite, using their knowledge.
- Ghostwriting non-fiction gives you the opportunity to learn new things.

8 | Ghosting the short stuff

One-minute overview

In this chapter
- Openings for short pieces
- Promotional articles
- When there's not enough for a book
- Letters
- Speeches
- Poems
- E-books
- I need a ghostwriter—advertisements
- Blogging

Openings for short pieces

There are many opportunities for ghostwriting when it comes to writing shorter pieces. These are increasing daily because of all the opportunities online. When reading anything online, from blogs to books, you can never be sure the goods have been supplied by the writer whose name is on them.

In the real world there are also plenty of openings for ghostwriting work. The trick is knowing where to find them. Hopefully, you will get ideas for ghostwriting work from this chapter.

Promotional articles

If you have ghostwritten a book you could also ghostwrite some promotional articles for your client.

My Husband Had 800 Gay Lovers. Does that, as a headline, grab your attention? This was the title of an article that one of my clients sold to a weekly women's magazine. At the time she was trying to generate some interest in her plight and phoned one of the tabloid magazines to offer her true life story. Later, that article helped her get my attention, and that of a few publishers, but if she had waited until her book had been written it would have generated fantastic publicity. Normally such an article would be written and offered for sale once the book was in print. It would help with sales. The magazine could have been asked to add a little bit about the book at the end of the article and readers, wanting to know more, might have searched it out and bought it.

Articles, like the above, written at the right time, are good for promoting your work. The magazine had been very clever using such an eye-grabbing title. Any woman seeing it would immediately start asking herself questions. Is she still married to him? Who is this woman? Did she know what was going on? Has she just found out? Is she still with him? 800??? Where did he find the time? They would turn to the page and read it through to discover the answers.

As the ghost it might fall to you to write the promotional article. Of course, the subject can simply phone the magazine using the number advertised in its pages, and recount the story to them for one of their writers to produce. The magazine would pay your client a fee for this but if you wrote it you have control over which elements of the story you want to reveal. Enough will be needed to make a complete and rounded article but you don't want to give away everything. When the magazine pays, according to whatever agreement you made beforehand with your client, you will receive a portion of the money.

If she contacts the magazine herself your client may give too much away. If they are interested in her story one of the magazine's experienced journalist may phone her and, by asking the right questions, will cleverly tease out more than your client will realise. It's their job to do this so it's no use complaining afterwards. If you act as your client's agent you will keep control of what is revealed and which aspects of her story are kept secret. If everything is given away in an article then what would be the point of reading the book? The same goes if you write the promotional article. You will almost definitely find changes made to it when it gets into print. Magazines have their own style and will change yours to suit.

> *'I checked the magazine's requirements and worked hard at the article I was ghosting. It was a tabloid magazine and if pushed to describe the writing style I'd have to say lurid. Once my job was completed I gave myself ten out of ten for achieving just that but when the piece appeared in print the editor had made many changes. I realised my ten had been a poor five, but I learned from those changes and will know better next time.'*
>
> Ghost 1

Be sure to use the juiciest most tempting bits to lure your readers into reading the article first, and then, wanting more, to get them to buy the book. There were plenty of juicy bits in this client's book. Spend time over the title. You need something that will make the editor zoom in on your piece, even if he or she changes it before it appears in print. Check out the titles of other real life stories in these tabloid style weeklies and dream up something that will fit. This could be one word or a phrase from the actual story. It will certainly be attention grabbing. You can see the sort of thing they want by checking out the front cover. *"Topping up the tank gave me an orgasm." "I woke up as the surgeon was slicing me."*

Not all books are of the kiss-and-tell or revenge types. If your book doesn't fall into that category you can still use promotional articles for stories of bravery, family loyalty, huge problems being overcome etc. but you still need to cherry pick the best bits of the book to use in such an article.

Clients may start off by telling you their story and end up with a book which also deals with self-help. Their story can be an example to others suffering in the same or similar ways. If your client wants to tell the story of how she and her partner coped when their child was born with spina bifida there will be the shock, the *"why me?"*, the dawning of what this disability will mean to the entire family and then, later, how they drew on strengths they had never dreamed they possessed.

Information on societies, websites, and help-groups may also feature in the book and, what had begun as a family story, could well turn into a book filled with good advice which would inspire and encourage other families in the same situation.

When there's not enough for a book

The experience of climbing a mountain might fill a book. There would be the initial idea, the actual learning to climb process, the preparation, the journey there, the adventures on the mountain and finally the reaching of the summit. But what if your client has had an experience that won't fill a book? What if they had saved a child from drowning, been a witness to an armed robbery, or had an operation that went wrong? What if they ask you to write their story and you know full-well that you can't string it out for 50,000 words?

If a prospective client has had a one-off experience that certainly won't fill a book then you could suggest writing it up as an article. Tell them that a short piece makes sense, will be easier to write, cost them less and be easier to sell. Then write it up for the magazines that use several real-life stories each week.

Other articles

If you are asked to write articles for a client who specialises in, let's say, homeopathy, then you may need to do some research for them. They may even expect you to help, or take over the researching responsibilities.

If your client wants to write for a specific market then ask him to supply a copy of the relevant magazine so that you can study the articles in it for length and style. Don't wait to be asked to come up with ideas for further articles. Suggest it yourself. Your client's name will be on the final pieces but, during this process, you may well have become a bit of an expert yourself. You and your client will reap the benefits. You get the work. They get the credit.

Letters

Writing letters for clients who cannot express themselves is nothing new. My very first ghostwriting was for a fellow pupil at school who wanted to write a love letter. I can't remember my client's name but have a strong suspicion that I was sworn to secrecy. The outcome of my purple prose has long been forgotten but I do remember one phrase I was especially proud of at the time—*My heart is on fire for you and only your kisses can quench the flames.* These may not have been *my* original words. Not knowing anything of plagiarism they may have been borrowed from another source. That letter was certainly a proper ghostwriting job though. I still remember the jam do-nut that was handed over as payment.

In the 1830s Becky Swann had a sign outside her house on Comberton Hill, Kidderminster. It stated–

> **Town and Country Letter Writer to All Parts,**
> **Gives advice in all periods.**
> **No need to apply without recommendation.**
> **I have been wrongfully used.**
> **Wishes to do justice, love mercy and**
> **Walk humbly with God.**

The last five lines refer to Becky's occupation as a white witch. It is the first sentence that is of interest. This woman offered her services as a letter writer. She could have classed herself as a ghostwriter because, for a fee, Becky would write letters on behalf of those who needed to send news to relatives but who could not write themselves. Many of Becky's contemporaries would have been illiterate so her services would have been appreciated. She was needed to write letters to be sent out and her services were required to read back any replies that were received. Being able to compose a letter by not only writing it but suggesting which words and phrases were needed was quite an accomplishment and probably a good source of income, for Miss Swann. And it didn't get her into as much trouble as the witchcraft did.

Letters of complaint

Letter writing is now a dying art form though you may be asked to produce one on behalf of a client who hasn't the necessary skills to complain. Letters of complaint can be lucrative and a share in the money might persuade you to take on a small job like this.

> '*Every time a corporate giant makes the slightest clerical error or offers less than impeccable service, I reach for the keyboard and make them wish they'd never messed with a writer,*' wrote a fulltime freelance journalist in *Writers' Forum*.

His advice is to write to the top, the big name who presides over the parent company, and this can be found on Google. '*Write a very long letter,*' he continues, '*spelling out exactly how big their cock-up was and the immense inconvenience it's caused you. Finally, make it clear that you not only want the mistake rectified but you expect financial compensation for your trouble. I've found that suggesting a figure works better than leaving it to their imagination.*

'*My biggest pay-out yet is £500 from my electricity supplier. Long story short—there was a voltage overload that left me without electricity for a day and also blew up my computer. They fixed the computer and replaced the monitor of their own accord, but I felt I deserved some compensation for stress, inconvenience, lost earnings etc, so I wrote to tell them so. If you want a big amount, ask for a big amount. In this instance I asked for £1000 and they settled for half of that.*'

I asked neighbours and friends if they would do this and the reply was almost always, "*I wouldn't know where to start.*"

It's difficult to get into a conversation these days without someone telling you of the poor service they've received. Next time a friend or acquaintance does so, take them to one side and propose a ghostwritten letter to them. Suggest that you will do it for a small fee or suggest you do it for free but will expect 50% of whatever is received as compensation from the company causing the hassle. Instead of whingeing, do something. Complain in writing if the problem is yours and always offer to complain (ghost) on someone else's behalf.

> **Make a note** – Don't switch off next time someone is moaning about a product or service. Listen carefully and see if their complaining offers you a little ghostwriting job.

Speeches

For most of the population giving a speech isn't an everyday occurrence. It's a big deal. They won't want to mess up a friend's wedding by stumbling through a few memories of the groom, or embarrass the guests by giving too much detail of the drunken stag night. This is the story of a shy person, let's call him Tony, whose life-long friend asked him to be best man at his wedding.

Tony panicked. He'd said yes and then, even though the wedding was several months away, he began to worry about what he was going to say in his speech. Organising the stag night, looking after the rings, toasting the bridesmaids, all that was easy compared to standing up in front of a hundred plus guests and delivering a speech. They'd expect him to be clever, witty, amusing. He started dreaming about the spectacular flop he would be. As best man he would ruin the wedding for everyone and never be able to show his face again.

Tony decided to visit the library and see if there were any books on wedding etiquette and hopefully the duties of a best man. What he really needed was a book telling him how to write an entertaining speech. He found several books about weddings. There was even one about being a best man but nothing on the shelves mentioned best man's speech. In desperation he approached a librarian, a fellow man. He would understand. The librarian didn't know of a book specifically about giving speeches at weddings though he plucked out a few on public speaking. Tony thought they looked a bit too business like for his needs. Then the librarian, who was a member of the same writers' group as me, suggested that Tony should contact a local writer who might be persuaded to write the speech for him. I was that writer.

I received a phone call from him one morning. He told me his problem and asked if I'd be prepared to help. What he really wanted was someone to ghost the speech for him. As a writer one of my mottoes, when it comes to writing work, is *"say yes first, think later."* I said yes. And I immediately mentioned a price. I suggested a café in the centre of town and we agreed a date and time to meet.

He was an extremely pleasant man, older than I had imagined, but very shy and unsure of himself.

We talked for a while before getting down to business. I asked him about his job and his home life. Gradually Tony began to relax. He told me the wedding arrangement, dates, times etc and I steered him into talking about the groom, how they'd met, how long they had known each other. I opened my notebook and made pages of notes. I had also switched on a small digital-recorder so that I would have a complete record of our conversation. I encouraged Tony to talk about the friendship he had with the groom and noted down some of the anecdotes he told me. He could go back to childhood days and there was an especially amusing story about a toy train and the two boys falling out over it. When we left the café I knew I had more than enough material for a speech. We arranged to meet a week later when I would have the written speech ready for Tony.

It took immense concentration on my part to transcribe the notes I needed from the recording. Our voices were drowned by the loud clashing of knives and forks, coffee being stirred, newspapers rustled, and a never ending thrum of background chatter. Memory and notes had to be relied upon.

A week later Tony and I met up again and nervously, I handed over the speech. Many writers will understand this feeling. It's not always a good idea to actually be present when someone is reading your work. On this occasion there was no need to worry. Tony laughed several times as he read through my pages. He was happy with what I had ghostwritten for him. I suggested he practised reading the speech in front of a mirror and gave him the idea of using props. Perhaps he could wave the toy train under the groom's nose when he reached that part of the speech. Tony still owned the train they had argued over as small boys.

My client folded the speech and placed it in his pocket and then he took out my fee, in cash, and counted it into my hand. Several customers on nearby tables appeared very interested in the transaction. We were in the window seat again and, as I looked away from them, a friend was walking past outside. She was about to wave when she saw money changing hands. Quickly she stared down at the pavement and sped past the window. Driving home I started to laugh, finally realising what the passing of cash might have looked like to outsiders.

Lessons

- Discuss prices first.
- Make sure your client knows that you will expect to be paid.
- Always arrange to meet strangers in busy places.
- Do not eat when interviewing a client; especially do not eat sticky foods.
- Put your client at ease before getting down to business.
- Do not rely on digital-recorders when interviewing in a public place as background noise can obscure the conversation.
- Make sure you have enough information from your client.
- Take a contact number in case you need to ask further questions, or need to check on information.
- Give yourself plenty of time to get the job done.
- Arrange to be paid discreetly.

After that experience I placed a small advertisement in the local paper, offering to write speeches. The next client arrived via that advertisement. This time around I knew the ropes therefore the whole experience was a lot easier. We arranged a meeting place, same café, different seat, and I made sure that I took lots of notes.

This client, another man, had been asked to give away a young friend at her wedding as she had no father. He was extremely honoured to have been asked and became quite emotional when he told me how it had come about. "*She's special,*" he kept repeating but it took a while to winkle out of him why this girl was so special. She was a friend to his own children and had become part of the family. She didn't have any special talents, he said, but as we talked further I discovered this girl's particular, and special, talent. When I put it into words he agreed that this is what he'd been trying, and failing, to say. "*That's it. That's exactly what she's like. That's what I was trying to tell you,*" he said.

This speech meant so much to him and he didn't want to let his *pretend* daughter down. He was not particularly articulate so care was needed in order to get his voice over in my words. I knew I had to do a good job.

My client has given permission for me to use his speech here, as long as the names are changed.

'I'm here today as Tracey's surrogate father. It's not a hard part to play because, since meeting Trace ten years ago, she has become like another daughter to me.

I know she's worried about what I might say but, Tracey, you can sit back and relax because I'm not going to say anything about your language during that terrible thunder storm, how much booze you can get through on a Friday night or any of your other little secrets.

I was really touched and honoured to be asked to give Tracey away today. Actually, as I'm self-employed, giving anything away goes against the grain. If Martin was an Arab I'd have got a couple of camels for her, at least.

Ten years ago Tracey walked into our lives. She was a friend of our kids and soon became our friend too. She was always ready to roll up her sleeves and tackle some work, be it unpacking and pricing stock, making cups of tea for us and the sales reps' or trying to serve customers—not easy when you know sod all about car parts.

The wife and I ended up taking her to University and fetching her home for the holidays. Tracey showed us how students live by dragging us around the student pubs and bars and taking us to all the cheapest places to eat. The journeys back and forth were always a pleasure. We'd laugh for miles while we played silly games, searching for one-eyed farmers driving tractors or cows with wooden legs. We even had an encounter of the third kind on one trip. Remember Beryl and Ethel, Tracey?

Tracey became an important part of our lives and we were delighted when she asked us to be at her Graduation ceremony. She's sent me a Father's Day card for many years now but doesn't realise how happy these make me. I've watched her grow from a young girl into a beautiful young woman and I'm as proud of her today as any real father could be. I'm sure that somewhere her grandparents are looking down on this and are just as proud.

Tracey once told us she had no talents. She couldn't do anything, couldn't sing, sew, draw or even cook. Well, I expect Martin would agree with that last one but I can't agree that she has no talent. She's got a very special one. Right from the start whenever Tracey walked into a room she brought a ray of sunshine with her. She has that rare gift of being able to make people feel brighter, happier just by being in her presence.

Gillian (Tracey's mother), you've done a good job of bringing her up. She's a credit to you and now you can pass the responsibility onto younger and stronger shoulders. Martin, she's all yours.

I hope you'll be very happy together. Well, you have been and I'm sure it'll continue.

Martin, here's a bit of advice for you. It's what my wife keeps telling me. Remember that an interesting woman is never easy to live with.

Now, would everyone raise their glasses in a toast to the bride and groom.'

It's the little touches that can lift a speech. As a ghost you need to listen to everything you are told. I was able to include humour in the personal details of the bad language during the thunderstorm and the drinking sessions on a Friday. More humour came with the quote direct from my client—*"as I'm self-employed, giving anything away goes against the grain."* There are lots of little bits in the speech which show that Tracey and my client had a special relationship—the way she helped with his work and those trips to and from University. The Beryl and Ethel incident wasn't explained because it was a private joke between them. The mention of Tracey's grandparents was important because they had meant such a lot to her but had both died the previous year. I also included a reference to her mother because this was a tribute to a single parent and I ended with a little joke. The special talent that Tracey had was mentioned and my client told me how it had struck a chord with the wedding guests. *"As I said that bit I could see everyone nodding,"* he told me.

The fee was small but the rewards for this particular work were so worthwhile.

Not long after the above client had asked me to write his speech for his *pretend* daughter's wedding, another father of the bride turned up. He told me how he was worried about making a speech as it would be a new experience for him, and then he'd become even more worried when his family kept saying they were expecting him to be funny. This had frightened him even more. We discussed his daughter and she sounded as if, to be polite, she'd been quite a challenging child. When I put this to the client he said, *"Oh, yes. You should see some of her school reports."*

My immediate reply was, *"I'd love to".* As it turned out those reports became the basis for the speech, a short and funny one, which was what the client had asked for. Here it is, with names changed:

'James, this is for you. Call it a dowry, if you like.
(I'd suggested he make up a parcel of the school reports,

the letter the headmaster had sent summoning the parents to the school when there'd been an incident, and any other paperwork he thought might be amusing for the groom to see.) *It's not to be opened now. I was going to leave the contents out for everyone to read but thought better of it.*

We were having a sort out and found some papers belonging to Sarah, including her school reports. They make interesting reading and, while I was looking at them, I noticed a few comments I thought should be passed on to my new son-in-law to prepare him for married life.

I don't know if you've been living on take-aways recently or whether Sarah does the cooking but her cookery teacher had this to say—"With a more determined effort Sarah could improve her practical cookery—there is plenty of room for improvement".

And another domestic subject—needlecraft. I hope you never need a button sewn on or your jeans turned up because, according to her needlework report, "Sarah places very little importance on this subject".

And one final warning. Save hard for the telephone bills. Over and over again the same phrases keep turning up from her teachers—"A very talkative pupil, she must curb her tendency to wander around the classroom chatting, Sarah loves to gossip". She once went on a school trip and met a boy from Australia. He gave her his phone number in Melbourne. We were too frightened to go out in case she called him for a two hour chat.

Sorry James, I suppose I should have warned you before but I didn't want to put you off. So, here you are (hand over the parcel), some reading material for the honeymoon.

I'd like to welcome you to the family and hope you'll be very happy.'

It was only because I had met the father and heard family stories that I knew this speech would go down well. This was a family who liked to tease each other and, as the father said, *"have a good laugh"*.

> **Make a note** – Place a small advertisement in the classifieds of your local newspaper, offering your services as a writer, and see what it produces. A regular inclusion will reap rewards.

You could soon find yourself ghosting speeches and letters. You never know what might turn up. I found some regular work this way. I concocted a couple of small advertisements and placed them alternately in the weekly newspaper. The first read, "*Speeches written for any occasion*" and the second, "*Poems produced for special occasions*". Naturally I included a phone number but left out my name and any other personal details.

Poems

Because of my regular small advertisements a businessman contacted me asking if I would write some light verse to add to his newspaper advertisements. He owned a garage and wanted me to write about the different makes of car he had for sale, extolling their virtues in rhyming verse or limericks. This man then passed these off as his own work. How do I know? I overheard an argument in a pub one night when his friends were telling him that he couldn't have possibly been the author. He was very convincing, insisting they were all his own work.

My poems weren't great works of art. They were often humorous and they always rhymed. They owed more to Pam Ayres than William Wordsworth.

I also found myself writing poems for wedding anniversaries, birthdays, births, students passing exams and learner drivers who had passed their tests. Clients would tell me a little about the person they wanted the piece written for and, in most cases, they passed my work off as their own. Interviews for little commissions like poems can take place over the phone.

You need to ask the five magic questions—Who, what, why, how, when and where.

Who is the poem for? It could be a partner, a friend, a family member. You will need to know the relationship and some relevant information about the recipient. What event is the poem needed for? Hatches, matches and dispatches are common. That is births, marriages and deaths. A funeral? Yes, I have a friend who writes beautiful poems for such occasions. Here is his story.

'People have really seemed to take to the idea of having some personalised poetry read out at the funeral of their loved one. My ghosting job began when I wrote for my cousin, who passed away, aged 52, earlier this year. He had acute myeloid leukaemia.

After my verse was read out in church I was approached by several people asking for me to do the same for their funerals, when the time came. Within a few weeks I'd been asked to write several and, as much as it gave me great pleasure to write these poems for free, I started to wonder if this was a service that people would pay for. Was it possible that there could be a market for a commissioned poem, as a way of summing up the lives/ characters of the dearly departed, as a tribute?

I produced a portfolio of fairly standard examples that could be adapted on request. Also, I advertised that I would take commissions for totally personal tributes, based on biographical and anecdotal detail.

£30 as an upfront charge, plus £15 per adapted verse, seemed a very good system because people can buy as much or as little as they want. Using this "bolt on" system, people were encouraged to keep adding verses, because they are only another £15 each. Before I knew it, I'd written eight verses, because each member of the family wanted something personal to contribute, and I netted £150. My name doesn't go on the verse. The name of the person who has paid for it does, so it can certainly be classed as ghostwriting.

People spend a fortune on flowers for all occasions. Something they can have forever—a poem—has got to be worth the same amount of money or even more.

I approached a couple of funeral parlours asking if I could leave some contact details about my services. I'm about to explore the possibilities of "advertising" with vicars and local churches and am wondering if there is some kind of bereavement liaison place in hospitals where I could put a card.

The verse is often accompanied by a picture. This may be of the deceased or of a flower or a favourite place. I print them out on good quality paper and offer to produce extra copies if needed. The client could photocopy their own copy but I'm often asked to produce one for each member of the congregation.'

More cheery subjects might include christenings, birthdays, engagements, jobs—leaving or getting a new one, moving to a new house, getting a divorce. In fact any subject covered by card companies could turn up for you as a ghostwriting commission.

Why do they want it? You need to find out why your customer wants the poem. Is it to say sorry, good luck, well done, I love you? Maybe it's a mixture of one or two things such as a parent wanting to say well done and I love you.

How long do they want it? Will four lines do? Perhaps a sonnet? Does it need to rhyme? Not necessarily though the answer to this is usually yes. The public tend to prefer rhyming verse.

How would they like it presented? You can print it out on gorgeous paper, use a fancy font, or print it on white A4 so the customer can copy it out in his or her own handwriting. You can add a suitable picture, a photograph, a mixture of both, several of each. Ask the client which they prefer and always give them what they want.

When does the client need the finished item by? It's very important that you have a deadline for little jobs like these. They will almost certainly all be needed for a specific date and if you miss the deadline you'll lose the fee and possibly any reputation you may have built up.

Where do you send the completed work? Does the client want it or do you send it directly to the person it has been written for. Always get as many details as possible when it comes to contacting your client. Write them down, check them and make sure you don't lose them.

Playing cupid

It's been years since I played Cupid and offered to write love poems for Valentine's Day. I had already prepared a few in the hope that they could be customised to suit. It turned out to be a good ploy. There were very few changes to be made as everyone wanted to say the same thing. I love you.

Now this type of service is offered on the internet. You could advertise yours this way or it might be worthwhile sending out an email offering your Cupid services to everyone on your mailing list. Even if they are other writers they might tell someone else about your idea and pass a client on to you.

Valentine's Day was a time of year when a special advert went into the newspaper. There are other times you could use too. Halloween poems might turn out to be a hit with the public. Then there's Easter, Christmas, New Year ...

Online dating services

Would you believe it? Here's another opportunity to ghostwrite. The upmarket online dating services which are used by professionals can be a market for ghostwriters. Apparently, setting up a profile and finding a date can be time consuming which is why some love-seekers employ someone to do the work for them. A ghost can offer to prepare their material, ready to go online. They can ghostwrite all of the communications between the two parties, search through the profiles and plan dates on behalf of their client. This is already acceptable in America so could well take on here. At the time of writing a basic match at Done For You Dating costs $147 but users only pay for an accepted match. The moral aspect of ghostwriting is covered in the final chapter.

E-books

More and more writers are turning to self-publishing. This is an excellent option for ghostwriters whose clients only want a few books printed, or for a subject which will not interest more than a few hundred people. E-books are another way to publish work. It's only an electronic version of a normal book and is read on an iPad, Kindle or other similar device.

With an e-book the agents and publishers can be by-passed. You don't have to pay for printing because there is no real, solid book to hold. This means it is cheaper. It can also be edited easily if any information in it needs changing or updating. And there are no boxes of books to hawk around shops. Everything, including sales, is done online.

As the popularity of e-books grows, more and more people will consider writing them. Some of those will be competent authors. Some will be complete novices who would need their work written for them. That's your job. And, if you are already ghosting a book and doubt its chances of being accepted by a mainstream publisher then turning it into an e-book could be the way to go for you and your client.

I need a ghostwriter — advertisements

Use Google and type in "online writing jobs". You will find pages of advertisements asking for ghostwriters for specific projects. In most cases you will be asked to bid for the work available. Remembering that this is the *world-wide-*web consider who you will be bidding against. There are countries, such as India, where there are competent writers who are happy to bid for what, to them, will mean a fairly decent income. What amazed me were the low bids that are put in to secure the work.

If you are serious about finding online ghosting work you should check these advertisements every day. You will have to apply for a lot of work and be prepared to be turned down. But if you keep at it your name will become known and companies regularly advertising will know that you can turn out good work, meet your deadlines and are trustworthy.

Try other search engines and, instead of "online writing jobs", try other words in the search subject. You could be vague:

- ghostwriting work
- ghostwriting jobs
- ghostwriters wanted

or you could be more specific and add your particular interests:

- ghostwriting articles
- ghostwriting novels
- ghostwriting life stories

Beware!

Are all of the advertisements legitimate? Are they for real? You have to read them carefully to find out.

If someone is asking for the services of a ghostwriter and mentions a grand sum as your expected share of the profits, beware. If you are a published writer you will know that many books do not even get into profit and there are authors out there whose books do not earn enough to cover their advances.

Another warning light is when the advertiser is talking about Hollywood films and best-sellers, believe me, it is unlikely. Even if a film company was to option the work the odds against it actually being turned into a film are still enormous.

Make sure that what is being offered is realistic and, whether the final product goes on to win glittering prizes and be featured on television channels around the world or sinks like Titanic, you are paid.

Interesting topics

Occasionally really interesting topics pop up. If I had lived in the right area I would have responded to a certain council in the UK who wanted someone to ghostwrite the history of a part of their town. The fee was £3000 and what was needed was set out clearly in the advertisement.

Another interesting advertisement was asking for a writer to assist in writing an historical romance. The advertiser admitted that they needed help with dialogue, descriptions and character analysis. The chosen ghostwriter would receive "*compensation, but no authorship rights, percentages or credits*". The ghostwriter would be paid by the page and would receive whatever they had earned on the completion of each chapter.

Another advertiser wanted a ghostwriter to write e-books about a specific topic. "*You will be writing as if you are the person mentioned in the bio provided ...*" it added. A sum for the 40,000 words needed was given. You want to know? OK. It was $750–$1500.

Replying to advertisements

You've found an advertisement that interests you. What do you do next? Go for it! Send a beautifully written reply. Be polite and make sure all your commas and stops are in place and your grammar is good.

Tell them that you are interested in the topic they want a ghost to write about and how you would enjoy writing about it. You need to convince them that you are perfectly capable and if the subject matter interests you, make sure you tell them so.

If you don't have a CV then you could offer to write so much for free. If you could send a well-written first chapter as an example of your work it could get you the job.

If you have to quote for the work then be sensible. If the work sounds easy enough, without too much research being involved, then send a fairly low quote but not a sum that will make you feel underpaid and undervalued. If this is your first time then it's worth asking the client how much he is willing to pay. If you don't get the work, or decide you don't want to work for that amount of money, you will still have gathered a little more experience.

Blogging

Larger companies, as well as some celebrities, want to have a blog about their business/life/forthcoming products or events etc.

The celebrities are too busy to blog regularly or feel inadequate about their writing skills. They want their blog to be interesting and to attract a following but can't think of enough subjects to write about and their words seem flat and uninteresting.

The businesses have to find someone to blog for them so pass the work to an employee whose heart isn't in it.

Now both are employing ghostwriters to blog for them. You may know of a company or you could try the online advertisements. If you were a life-long fan of a band member you could mention this and offer to post blogs for him, for a fee.

Businesses will give a ghostwriter notes about research, products and any ideas they may have and let the ghost do the work for them. It saves the business time and they know that they will be getting a professional writer to blog for them.

Smaller business, even one-man-bands, could be willing to employ you as a blogger. If one man is the sole owner, worker and PR for his business it would make sense for him to pay a professional to blog, and thereby free up his own valuable time. A good blog which attracts attention will also attract new customers. Try telling that to a few of your overworked self-employed friends.

Points to remember

- There are plenty of openings for magazine articles.
- Your client gives you the information and you write the article.
- Poems and speeches are always in demand.
- Small ghostwriting jobs can bring in regular money.
- Keep an eye on online opportunities for ghostwriting.

9 Ghosting fiction

Safer than truth

Some stories, such as the one I ghosted for Pat, are better as fiction. Pat's story would have worked as a novel and there would have been no need to employ a solicitor to check the copy and make sure that we could not be sued for anything said. Pat had been surrounded by rich and powerful men who had dreadful secrets. If her story had been fictionalised we could have included many more details but, as a factual account it was too dangerous to do so. It would have been a far easier, and safer option, to fictionalise the entire story and naturally, all the characters in it.

The innocent and the guilty

By fictionalising someone's life you can avoid libel by not naming the guilty. You give these people new identities, new faces and names, new places to live, change their ages—in short, make them unrecognisable.

The same goes for the innocent. If a woman wanted to write about her past but it held secrets that none of her family knew of she could ask a ghostwriter to fictionalise it for her. As an example, perhaps many years ago she gave away a child born out of wedlock, or she had to make a living as a prostitute, and has since risen in the world, she would be protecting not only herself but all the family members who had no clue about her past history. Her story will still get out there for the public to read but as a work of fiction it will protect the innocent from being hurt.

I've got a story for you

Has anyone ever said that to you? It often happens once you admit to being a writer. People will often tell you they have an idea for a great story or book but they can't write it themselves. More often than not it's their life story but the highs and lows which mean so much to them probably won't interest a publisher or many readers. I've heard tales of awful mothers-in-law trying to manipulate their sons and interfering in the marriage. Those won't make a book unless something terrible happens such as the mother-in-law being murdered. A friend often tells me I should write her story. It's an ordinary tale of a woman who has had a couple of failed marriages and a few affairs in-between. Each break-up has obviously been traumatic for my friend but wouldn't be of interest to anyone who doesn't actually know her, and most of those who do have probably already heard her tales of woe. There have been, are, and will be many more women in the same position. Once again, there would need to be something out of the ordinary in the story to attract any attention or the person whose story it is needs to be in the public eye. A household name will almost certainly find a publisher.

However, any of the above might be the start of a fictional piece. A good ghost can add the interest to the basic facts of their client's story. Not every client will agree to their story being passed off as fiction but a wise ghostwriter will know what to fabricate and when to use the real thing as fact. Other clients will get excited at the thought of their experiences being turned into a novel. If they need a little persuading you can always suggest you make them younger, taller, slimmer, and more beautiful/handsome. That would work for me.

> '*I was approached by a top business man who wanted to write about the industry he was involved in and the people who were dishonest within it. He had written a ten page outline of his experiences and said they were fictionalised but the main characters were easily recognised. Even I guessed who one of them was. He had barely disguised any of them and even when changing their names had kept to the original initials. The lifestyles, cars, and women these men were married to, and the women they were conducting affairs with, would have given the game away and he would have found himself in court. Luckily, after writing the outline he had realised that writing was more complicated and time-consuming than he had imagined and he asked me to complete the novel. It didn't take much persuasion to get him to agree to change everything—business, names, cars, location. Whether this book ever sees the light of day remains to be seen.*'
>
> Ghost 9

Sharing fiction

How do you go about ghosting fiction? The idea could be handed to you. This is from an email I received.

> *'I have always loved reading sagas and have come up with lots of ideas for writing some. I think whilst I have lots of value to put in, I really need help as this is the first thing I've written.'*

Once you advertise your ghostwriting services you too could receive an email like this. Then comes decision time; what do you do? I asked to see what the prospective client had already written. It so happened that she had made a good stab at the whole book and it only needed some revision, copy editing and a bit of moving around so that the book was in the right order. Instead of ghostwriting it for her I offered to copy-edit and proof read it. As she said later, "*The story was there but I needed you to bring it to life.*"

An explanation of copy editing is given at the end of this chapter.

What if a prospective client turns up with an idea for a novel and it is just that—the idea? If it's a good one and you feel it's worth going along with then you treat it as any other ghostwriting job. There needs to be a discussion and a contract before work begins. Ask your client for any written notes he or she may have made. Make voice recordings or notes yourself of everything they think they want to include in their fictional work. Then take some time out to mull it over. Will it work as it is? Does it need further thinking, more characters, a few more plotlines?

Once again it is up to the two of you to decide how to set about working. The client could be happy to give you an extensive outline and allow you to get on with the work. Or they might want to be included in the writing sessions. Who would want anyone peering over their shoulder as they type up each chapter? Not me, for sure. If that's the way the client wants it and you can cope then do so. Otherwise you could suggest working together on a chapter at a time then the client goes away and you call them when you have completed the chapter so that you can get together for a read through and discussion.

What if they don't like your version?

You have to explain that you are the writer, the expert and you know how to write and how the writing business works. If, for example, they want a character to do something that you consider it is not in their personality to do then you need to get this across in plain words. If you explain clearly and carefully, hopefully the client will come around to your way of thinking. If they don't then you bring out the big guns and tell them that if you go their way then the book will have little chance of seeing the light of day, or you threaten to give up on the project. On some occasions, such as three quarters of the way through the writing of a book, it is worth remembering that old adage, the customer is always right.

Could women's magazine stories be written like this?

To ghostwrite a short piece of fiction such as a short story for a women's magazine would be a great apprenticeship for ghosting longer fiction. One thousand words will be far less stressful than one hundred thousand. The same rules would apply. Meet the client, discuss the project, listen to the client's ideas and then write the work for them, under their name, and for an agreed share of the profits if, or when, the story is accepted and published, or agree a set fee to cover your time. The latter ensures you don't work for nothing.

Celebrities writing novels?

Many actors are multi-talented and could be perfectly capable of turning out a best seller all by themselves but what of the celebrities who aren't? A lot use ghostwriters to turn out their fiction for them.

There is a lot of controversy over celebrities writing novels when these novels have been ghosted. Some have even won prizes. When the work sporting their name, usually in large letters, has been ghosted the question arises, is this fair? Think of it this way. Would you turn down an offer to ghostwrite a novel for a well-known name when the book is guaranteed to sell well, simply because of the name on the cover? It would mean a lucrative deal for any ghostwriter and the publisher will make a profit too.

The truth is that many of the reading public will pick up that book and buy it simply because it says it is by one of their favourite pop stars, actors, television celebrities … Some of those people may not be regular readers and, it could be said, that reading the novel written by their favourite celebrity might persuade them that reading is a good hobby. They might even start buying books by *real* authors. Is this me looking on the bright side or could such a thing happen? Isn't it more likely that the new reader will be put off by the novel? After all, it must sound as if the celebrity has written it themselves but does that automatically mean that it will not be a good read? Or at least be enjoyed by those members of the public who want light and frothy?

For those of us who have learned our craft and know what it is like to sit down and write a novel it is difficult to see a pretty starlet smile at the television cameras and say, "*It were hard sitting there until I'd wrote a thousand words every day*," or words to that effect.

We know it's not just a case of sitting down to churn out a certain number of words.

It was back in 1994 that a novel appeared bearing Naomi Campbell's name. Later she admitted she'd never even read it. The novel was simply another product that was being sold with her name on, exactly the same as dresses or perfume would be.

Novels by Katie Price have, as we all know, been ghostwritten and have sold, together with her multi-autobiographies, over three million copies. No wonder there was a mad dash of celebrities wanting to get a novel like Jordan's out there on the bookshelves.

Team fiction

Have you seen the long rows of children's books in WH Smith's or Barnes and Noble—the ones that are all about a certain subject, person or animal and there are so many that they have numbers on the spine? They are numbered because children like to collect them and they know which numbers they have and which they still want. The books have an author's name on the spine but, in most cases, this author is as fictional as the talking dog, or little girl destined to become a world famous ballet dancer, that features inside the covers. Many of these series books become so popular that one author would not be able to keep up with the demand. A team of writers do the work and produce the books. They are actually ghostwriting for a non-existent person.

These books are easy reads, have simple plots and happy endings. They are the sort that a lot of parents or grandparents will read to their children and state, "*I could have written that*". As writers we know that the work that looks simple and is easy to read has taken a lot of hard work and effort on the part of the writer.

My experience of team fiction was short lived. I was invited to try out for a team of writers who were producing stories about animals. *"What do you know about horses?"* asked my agent. *"They have a leg on each corner,"* was my reply and apparently that was all the knowledge I needed. When researching the books I realised why these qualifications were enough. The horses in question all chatted to each other and had wonderful adventures which would make most human lives seem boring by comparison.

I was given a three line synopsis of what my story should be about and, after reading a dozen of these books, set to work.

The first page took ages to write as I worked hard to craft every word so that it was in the same style as that of the fictional author then, suddenly I was away, fingers flying over keyboard, absorbed in the plot. Five pages later I stopped to look over Chapter One. Page one was almost there but after that everything needed deleting.

Page one was in the style of the fictional author, the rest— the part that had flowed—was in my style. I tried again, and again and could never get the style right. It was so completely different to my natural style and was, in fact, one that I downright disliked—that of talking down to the child.

At that point in my career I was not very experienced. Now I would have tried much harder and achieved what the publishers wanted.

Later I learned that schools often invited the author of these books to speak to their pupils. If one had been within my area I would have been asked to go along as the author's representative. As the author was supposed to be a man the kids would have had a surprise when they saw me walk into their classroom. I wonder how, *"He's too busy writing to come, so he's sent me,"* would have gone down? That's rather like going to a large store to see Father Christmas and having an elf sitting there saying, *"The boss is having a day off but you can tell me what you want for Christmas. I'm Santa's little helper."*

To get into team writing you will almost certainly need an agent who works for the publishers who produce this type of book. They can put your name forward as someone who is interested in team writing but beware. Your work would have to sound exactly like all the other members of the team and many writers give up because their stories are returned over and over again, asking for changes and wanting revisions. It has to be perfect.

Anna Bowles writes series fiction. This is where several writers produce books set in the same world and a publisher releases them under a single pseudonym. The *Nancy Drew* books and the *Hardy Boys* books were written that way and, more recently, *Rainbow Magic*. She says that collaborative series fiction seems to be a growth area at the moment.

Writing for licensed characters

Anna Bowles is a prolific writer but does not have her name on much of the work she writes. She says:

> 'Technically it's not ghostwriting but it requires a lot of the same skills. It's generally fairly easy to capture the voice of a preschool TV character, but writing rhyming couplets in the tradition of classic Rupert Bear, for example, is a meatier challenge. I'm not Alfred Bestall (Rupert writer and illustrator from his heyday) and I'm not pretending to be, but Rupert's adult fans wish I was and it's my job to sound as much like the original as possible, while subtly updating the feel of the text.
>
> Conventional ghostwriting, such as writing the autobiography of a celebrity, requires sustained ego-submersion and the adoption of a particular single voice. I don't have to do that per se, but I do write in dozens of different fictional worlds that are not of my own making. Versatility is a key skill, as is a willingness to completely rewrite everything five times if the licence-holder of the TV show doesn't like your work. With licensed publishing there's no secrecy aspect to who writes the books, it just tends not to be on the cover because eight-year-olds don't care.

The closest thing I've done to pure ghostwriting is the Hello Kitty Annual, which is written in the first person, from Hello Kitty's own perspective. But I imagine most readers will realise that the book was not, in fact, written by a cartoon character, and that there must be a person behind it somewhere.

Sometimes I am credited as the writer or mentioned in the acknowledgement, but it's the exception rather than the rule. I'd estimate that my name appears in small print in the front matter of about a fifth of the books I've written. It's not that the credit is going to someone else, it's just that the readers don't care who wrote them. It's my job to merge absolutely into the brand.

I've written for a very wide range of characters now. I guess the top ten would be Wallace and Gromit, Thomas the Tank Engine, Ben 10, Hello Kitty, Star Trek, Rupert Bear, Winnie-the-Pooh, Barbie, Shaun the Sheep and Lazytown. My output can be as simple as a children's activity book or as complicated as a large-format hardback book with novelty elements and pop-ups. I've occasionally had to write an activity book in a single day (not recommended, admittedly), but then something like My Journey with Thomas the Tank Engine, which is a folder-format novelty with extras, like a passport and postcards, took hundreds of hours of development. Like conventional ghostwriters, I have sales figures to my name rather than publicity—books I've written have sold over two million units.'

How did Anna get into writing for licensed characters?

'Very much via an editorial route. My first editorial assistant job was working on licensed magazines like X-Files and Star Trek at Titan Publishing. When I left there, I began writing freelance articles for the magazines, though they were generally features about the shows rather than writing in the voice of characters. I started writing books when I became an editor at a children's publisher. I suppose that sounds odd, or at any rate doesn't fit most people's ideas of the industry!

But licensed publishing has a different business model to regular books, because you're paying the copyright holder of the TV show for the right to use their brand, and that doesn't leave much money for hiring an author. So for shorter children's books the text is often written in-house. For example, a recent freelance stint at a major publisher as Senior Editor saw me writing three books.'

Copy editing

Copy editing involves making the copy clear. It has to read well and be concise and also correct. It also requires you to check all spelling, grammar and punctuation. You will need to read carefully and make notes to ensure that the timelines are right and that for books that deal with history, words used are the correct ones for the era the book is set in. You can cut and polish for the client, removing superfluous words and phrases or even whole pages or paragraphs. What you are doing is ensuring that the book is as good and correct as it can possibly be. The text needs to flow naturally and all facts must be accurate. You will also need to check that there is nothing in the book which might lead to a problem, such as legal action being taken against the publisher and/or writer.

Points to remember

- True life can also be fictionalised, and sometimes it's safer that way.
- As a ghostwriter you can help others achieve their ambitions.
- There is no type of fiction that cannot be ghostwritten—crime, children's writing, romance, adventure …
- Ghostwriters can also produce short stories for clients.

Selling the story

One-minute overview

In this chapter
- Big names sell books
- Getting *ordinary* lives into print
- Agents
- Publishers
- Proposals
- Deadlines
- Self-publishing

Big names sell books

Actually big names sell anything and everything. We've seen adverts for perfume, fizzy drinks, make-up, hair colourants, holidays, all sorts featuring the latest name from the world of pop music or modelling, the current favourite footballer or the latest actor—anyone who appears regularly on our screens or in our newspapers or magazines. Not all accept but many have been offered contracts to promote products.

It's the same with books. If the person featured in the book is well-known then the public will want to read it, whether it's the ghosted autobiography or the ghosted novel or children's book by their favourite celebrity. It's not perfect but it is what the world is like at the moment and we need to accept those facts. Celebrities are themselves often promoted as products.

Easier to sell a name

If you are lucky enough to ghost for a celebrity then you will be able to attract the attention of publishers and agents. Sales will be good and, because of the name you are writing for there will be the opportunity for the book to be promoted on television and in magazines.

Getting *ordinary* lives into print

These can often be the most interesting and fascinating even if no-one has ever heard of your client but that alone won't get you a contract. If you are ghostwriting for an unknown then you will need to explain the publishing world to them. Point them in the direction of their nearest book store and ask them if they can find any autobiographies there that are written by *ordinary* people. The answer will almost definitely be no, unless the store has a few copies of self-published work by local authors.

Some ghostwriters undertake to write the book and nothing else. They do not offer to find a publisher and make no promises that the finished item will become a published book. Once the work is handed over it is up to the client to find a publisher for themselves. You can give advice and point them in the right direction as this ghostwriter did;

> 'My client took no notice of the advice and the model letters to agents and publishers that I gave him. He went straight to a vanity publisher. They made a very good job of his book but it cost him and I think he may still have a bedroom full of copies.'
>
> Ghost 2

There is nothing to say that you won't get a contract for your book with a mainstream publisher or a small independent, but be realistic and explain the realities to your client. Prepare them for rejection and let them know that the only certain way to see their work in print is to self-publish or produce it as an e-book.

Agents

If, as a writer, you have an agent then they are first port of call. Why not let them know you have taken on a project to ghostwrite for a client. Ask if they would be interested in taking a look at the work. You never know. They might know of a publisher who would be interested. If not, it was worth a try.

If you don't already have an agent is it worthwhile trying to find one? The answer to that would be yes, if your story is good enough or interesting enough. Grannies and egg sucking apply again here but there are lists of agents to be found in *The Writers' and Artists' Yearbook* and *The Writers' Handbook*. Each book holds information about what subjects each agent deals in. Don't go sending your misery memoir to an agent dealing exclusively in children's books.

> 'Once I'd finished the book, I then set about finding a specialist non-fiction agent, as my fiction agent didn't think she'd be able to place the book. He's been putting projects my way ever since ...'
>
> Lynne Barrett-Lee

Publishers

If you don't have an agent or don't want to use yours because this is a completely different aspect of writing to what you normally do then you can try going directly to a publisher. Once again you need to select the right one by once again studying *The Writers' and Artists' Yearbook* and/or *The Writers' Handbook*. If you think you have a good enough story to sell to a mainstream publisher then send them a brilliant proposal and a title that will grab their attention. Don't send to one and sit back and wait for a response. Send your proposal out to as many publishers as you can find that fit the bill. Multiple submissions are normal procedure now. Let each publisher or agent know that you have sent the same proposal to others.

Proposals

If you've ghosted a novel then you need to send in whatever the publisher asks for. They might want the first three chapters and a synopsis. Or they might ask for random chapters. I recently heard of a company who, instead of a synopsis, asked for a blurb—the bit on the inside cover of a book that gives the gist, or overview, of the story in a couple of hundred words at the most, and makes you want to read it.

You can find submission guidelines on publishers' websites. These will tell you exactly what is required.

You should always be honest when dealing with publishers so you will need to explain that you have ghosted the novel for a client.

If you need an outline or synopsis some tips are given in this chapter.

If you have ghosted a life story or a non-fiction book you will need to send the publisher a proposal.

This is your sales pitch. In it you need to get over how good your book is. This is your one chance to do so and if your proposal doesn't catch a reader's eye then it's not going to be passed up the line until it reaches the people who really matter—the ones who decide whether to take the book on or not. A proposal will consist of:

- an outline of the book.
- chapter contents.
- a CV.

Outline

Synopsis or outline? Are they different? The dictionary says that a synopsis is a condensed statement or outline (of a narrative). It also says that an outline is a condensed treatment of a subject. The important word here is *condensed.* Condensed means to make more compact. You need to compact a complete book into one page of narrative. Does this sound impossible? It's not but anyone who has ever written one will tell you it's not easy. It may be short but it can be the most difficult part of the book to write. It needs to be short because you are dealing with busy people who don't have the time to read every book that is sent in. They rely on reading a proposal, a synopsis, even a brilliant blurb—anything that grabs their attention and makes them want to know more.

For inspiration, and guidance, check out the blurbs on book covers. These are well written, often only a couple of paragraphs but those few words are designed to draw you in and make you want to know more about the book. This is what your job is when writing an outline.

Ideally your outline should fit on one page of A4. Include the title and setting. Where is your story set, and when? Who is it about? Obviously you will need to introduce your main character. If this is a ghosted autobiography then you need to give information to make this person sound interesting, interesting enough to warrant having a book published about their life. For instance:

Elaine Carson had a husband, children and a good job but an accident left her with no memories. She couldn't even remember how to speak.

It's a daunting task to summarise your entire book onto one page. Try writing down the main facts of the story and then keep working with them until you have a proposal that is going to sound exciting and stand out from a hundred other proposals.

If it's a ghosted novel then, in one short sentence, say what your story is about.

This is the story of Emma who, via her blog, pours out her concerns about what is going on in her neighbours' cellar.

Next, introduce your hero or heroine and main characters by name, giving their ages and jobs if such things apply. You need to make them sound real, alive and interesting. Add details about the family if they feature in the story. Keep it short.

What sort of book is this? Sci-fi, adventure, crime, romance? You should also include your 'theme' here. Do you have something special to say in your story? All of this needs to sound exciting. You are trying to sell a book which is a page-turner.

You could include one or two important scenes from your book but don't go into full detail. Write them as tempters. Make the reader want to know more so they will ask to see the complete manuscript.

One single sentence should be enough to show how a dramatic moment, possibly the most dramatic moment in the book, affects your main character. This could be the turning point in your story.

Now for the final scene; could you use the last sentence in the book to show the satisfying ending?

By the time you've done this everything should be covered but if you think there is something else which needs to be included do so now. Do it in another single sentence.

> And now it's time to go back to the beginning and start rewriting. Make your sentences shorter, crisper, more alive. Take out any extra words. Re-arrange sentences so that the whole piece reads well. Tinker until you are satisfied.

Chapter contents

In your proposal you will need to include a chapter outline. You have more space to spread yourself with this one. You will have given your chapters numbers or titles, or both. Under each of these give a brief outline of what is included in each chapter. Some authors recommend that this is written in the present tense to give a sense of pace. Treat each chapter outline as flash fiction—a short, short story.

CV/ resumé or biography

When ghostwriting life stories you need two CVs/resumés. Yours and that of your client and that's why I've used the word biography. These aren't details of which schools you went to and what jobs you've both held since.

Your CV/resumé will show the publisher that you are a professional writer. It will list your achievements, especially those relating to similar types of work to the one you are submitting. There's no need to include everything. They don't need to know how many household tips or jokes you've sold to women's magazines. What they want is proof that you are a competent writer.

Publishers will need a very short biography of your client giving the details that are relevant to their story. Make it interesting so that it holds their attention. Keep it short. Keep it simple. And stick to the point.

Deadlines

Writers know all about deadlines. We love them and hate them. Love because having a deadline means you have some commissioned work to do. Hate because the deadline looms far away on the horizon for a long time, unmoving, yet suddenly it races towards you and no matter how hard we try most writers find themselves having to speed up work in order to reach their deadline.

If you're lucky enough to get interest in your project and secure a contract then you will have a date for delivery—a deadline. It is vital that you get your client to realise how important that deadline is. It's not a date that can, or should, be changed. Deadlines are there for a reason. If, for any reason, you don't think you will be ready on time let your publisher know as soon as possible, even if you only think you might be late. Writers understand deadlines. Their customers don't.

When ghostwriting for a client who doesn't have a publishing contract it is still a good idea to impose a deadline otherwise you may discover that the client's other work, family life etc take up all of their time and the project drags on endlessly.

Self-publishing

Self-publishing is perfectly respectable now and it is getting cheaper and more easily available all the time. There are print on demand companies so there is no longer any need to order a shed load of books which may not sell. These print on demand companies allow the client to have as many or as few copies of his work as he wants. This is ideal for a client who simply requires a dozen copies of his memoirs to give to family members.

The reasons for choosing self-publishing are many and varied. If your subject doesn't attract a mainstream publisher or a small independent, you could consider this route. Some life stories and certain subjects will have a limited market so won't attract the major companies.

There are many books and articles written about self-publishing and if this is the way ghost and client prefers to go then it would be wise to read up on the subject and check out some websites for further information. Technology changes all the time and it changes quickly. By the time you read this there may be newer and even more inventive ways of getting into print.

One of the major points to take into consideration when self-publishing is the sales and promotion of the book. All of that will be down to the client, the ghostwriter, or both, depending on what was decided at the beginning when a contract was set out.

Many amateur writers use self-publishing as a way into print, and you can tell. Often the quality and content of the writing is poor. When your client goes down the self-publishing route he, and you, will know that your book looks and reads like a professional job.

Points to remember

- Ghostwriters get paid whether the book is published or not.
- Ghosts can choose whether to get involved in the search for a publisher.
- Writing a proposal is never easy but spending time on it pays dividends.
- There is plenty of advice in books and online when it comes to self-publishing.

11 Afterwards

One-minute overview

In this chapter
- The finished item
- Selling and promotion
- Brainstorming
- Get over it!

The finished item

The finished item will be one of two things. You have completed the manuscript and are in a position to hand it over to the client or, if you have gone the whole way, the printed book has arrived. You can pick it up, hold it, open its pages and feel proud of a job well done. It is someone else's story but the words are yours and it is you who has done the bulk of the work. Congratulations!

Now is the time to let go. Your job is finished and hopefully you have another project waiting to be started, or already in progress.

For your client this is a huge moment. It could even be a life's dream come true and the book, to them, will feel like their property. It is, after all, their story. Have a drink together, have a party. Celebrate the achievement. A celebration is more likely to happen if your client is an unknown. If they are well-known they may not want you, the ghost, at their party. They may be passing the work off as their own and not be up for sharing the congratulations.

If you have decided to go further and help your client with publicity and sales you may still find yourself taking a back seat. It is your knowledge that the client needs now. They will want to know how to go about getting book signings, how to hold a launch party and how to get their book into shops.

Selling and promotion

Who does what? Is the ghost involved? These questions should have been agreed upon at the start of the venture. Many ghosts hand over the finished product and it's up to the client to find a publisher, or to self-publish and go on to promote and sell their own book.

You, as the expert, could give advice on how to go about selling and promoting. Newspapers and magazines, TV and radio all need considering, whether it be local outlets or national. Remember that this is all new territory for your client and the whole experience might go to their head.

> 'She messed up by putting important people's backs up. A respected journalist asked to meet her and she ordered the most expensive champagne at a meeting which only warranted coffee, and expected it to go on his expenses. That particular client did not endear herself to her interviewer.'
>
> Ghost 1

Can you trust your client not to mess up and get carried away when being interviewed? If a journalist suggested lunch would your client act professionally or irresponsibly? You could give them some guidance.

Book signings, author events and launch parties all sound extremely glamorous to the public whereas we writers know they all entail careful preparation and hard work.

> 'I organised for our local Waterstones to sell the book. I also contacted the local newspaper and the radio to tell them that there was to be a book signing. My client went on radio to give an interview which we had rehearsed beforehand with me being the radio interviewer and asking questions I thought might crop up. All went well but it was very strange to stand in the bookshop and watch my client signing, with a flourish, the book I had written.'
>
> Ghost 10

> *'My client was asked to appear on several chat shows. She gave a good account of herself in front of the cameras and always clutched a copy of her book in her lap, waving it about whenever the opportunity arose. On several occasions she invited me to go with her. Once I found myself sitting in the green room being handed sandwiches and coffee while I watched her on the TV set but there was never any chance that I would be there with her on the interviewer's couch.'*
>
> Ghost 1

The important thing for your client to know is that selling is vital and it's normally not part of the ghostwriter's job. This is the time you give them some tips and wave them on their way.

But what if you have agreed to help out with book sales? Think back to how you promoted your ghostwriting business. Many of those ways will come in useful when promoting the books. Once the book is ready the buzz word is sales.

Brainstorming

Whether you are helping your client, with the sales or not, you could have one final session together to do some brainstorming. It is very unlikely that your client will know what to do next so a few minutes or an hour spent telling them how they could promote the book would be a good idea. There is no reason you should get involved if you don't want to but some clients may need a little guidance and maybe some hand holding. You could type up some useful tips for your client and happily leave the rest up to them.

Launch parties

If your client is passing off the whole work as their own then you probably won't be invited but you could suggest to them that they don't spend too much money, unless money isn't a problem for them. The idea of a launch party is not simply to celebrate the birth of the book, it's to start selling copies of the book and who better to begin with than faithful friends and family members.

> '*I rely on the launch party to do exactly what it says in the name—launch the book. I would hope that everyone invited would buy a copy and have it signed by the author. These sales provide a good starting point.'*
>
> Ghost 7

If twenty people were to attend a book launch and each buys a copy and reads it then there are twenty people out there who could be recommending your work to others as a good read and thereby generating more sales.

Sales

Explain how important sales are to your client and, if they've self-published then they need to know that the arrival of the printed books is not the end of the work but the beginning of a completely new project. They will need to take their books out to book shops and any other places that might agree to sell on their behalf.

Even if you have managed to get a deal with a mainstream publisher for your client it is up to the client to do as much selling and promoting as possible.

Think outside of the box here. Book shops aren't the only outlets. A good salesperson will consider all sorts of outlets. Private shops, like your local newsagent, may take a few copies for their shelves. Ask the client who they know and who could help promote sales. Books crop up in all sorts of places—bike shops, hairdressers, swimming pools. Wherever your client goes they should ask if they could leave a few copies on a sale or return basis.

> '*I had ghosted a short book on cycle routes and the places of interest on those routes. My client turned out to be an excellent salesman and took copies to every cycle shop within a hundred mile radius. He would leave a few copies together with a self-addressed stamped postcard*

> *so that the shop proprietors could let him know when*
> *they needed more copies.'*
>
> Ghost 8

I've heard of writers selling their books in pubs, on cross-channel ferries, at fetes … The opportunities are endless if your client is willing to get out there and do the work. Be aware that some venues will expect a cut of the profits. Ten per cent is the most you should agree to.

Book signings

Your client may be confident, used to being in the public eye and therefore not need your support. Or they could be entirely new to being on public view and be shaking in their boots. In other words they may or may not need you to hold their hand when it comes to book signings.

Being a ghostwriter means going to a book signing without a pen! You don't really need to be there and often the *writer* may not want you there.

I remember standing at the back of the shop trying to be invisible—as ghosts are. It felt strange to watch my client sign the book I had written. It was my first ghostwritten book and I hadn't expected to feel almost jealous of the attention she was getting. The whole morning was probably made worse because the signing was taking place in my home town, not hers, and friends from my writing group had all turned up to buy copies. Once the signing was over, the author disappeared and I and my friends went to the pub for a drink. It was while we were there that their books were produced for me to add my signature to.

> *'I was warned that I would not be invited to the launch*
> *or any of the book-signings. Other ghostwriters told me*
> *that is the norm'. None of the four authors for whom I did*
> *honours wanted me there. The publishers were definite*
> *about it. Stay away—don't even creep in to a book-*
> *signing. I don't even have a signed book by one author.'*
>
> Ghost 3

> 'We had a wonderful launch party where I was introduced to the guests as the wonderful friend who had helped write the book.'
>
> Ghost 8

> 'I'm a professional. I don't expect to get the credit. I expect to get the money.'
>
> Ghost 1

Interviews

Once again local newspapers and the local radio station will be interested in a book launch. The name hasn't lost its glamour from when, years ago, authors were collected and chauffeur driven to their book launch parties which were paid for by the publisher. A piece in the local paper, together with a photograph can generate interest and, hopefully, sales.

Your client does the interviews but, once again, you can help them by supplying a few tips. These have been covered before but it's always a good idea to recap.

- Don't let them give the story away otherwise what would be the point of buying the book?
- Dress and decorum. Remind them that they are on show so they should look good and preferably not show themselves up by getting drunk. It has been known.
- Your client is not there purely for enjoyment. The task at hand is to promote the book. It's all about sales.

Talks

Your client may not be able to write but are they capable of giving a talk? Writing their life story was beyond them but that doesn't mean they cannot tell people about sections of it—enough for the listeners to want to know more and buy a book.

Ghostwriters often work for people who are articulate and charismatic and, even if not well-known, they could be perfectly able to hold the attention of an audience. Many groups are always on the look-out for speakers and your client could get a fee or a free dinner as well as have the opportunity to sell books. If the client is happy for others to know that you assisted them in the writing you could do talks together or you could take them on yourself but make sure you are not doing this for nothing, Always remember that you are a professional and professionals need paying.

> After ghostwriting a novel for a client the ghost turned up at a talk given by him.
>
> *'The author went to great lengths to describe how he came up with the plot, how many words he wrote per day etc. And then he suddenly spotted me sitting smiling at a nearby table! He turned bright red and completely lost the plot for the rest of his speech. Not that he would have ever had a plot without considerable input from me—and the daily word count was all mine!'*
>
> Ghost 3

Get over it!

The book is in print. The client is happy and working at selling. Your job is done and it's time to move on to the next project.

It took me a while to get over the horror of my client's story. The shame she felt had somehow rubbed off onto me. Several years later I read parts of the book again and was pleasantly surprised at the job I had done considering it was on such a difficult subject.

> *'The best moment of the whole experience was when I finished it! The sheer relief! But, I would do it all again. Many times I almost gave up on this one project, but I am glad I didn't.'*
>
> Julia Anderson

'When the ms was complete, we met up again and I handed him two hard copies and a disk, and signed the rights over to him. And that was that!'

Chriss McCallum

'There were times when we could have cheerfully murdered each other. I made a lot of mistakes but learnt more. A plus side was that I learnt the ins and outs of how to write a decent book proposal.'

Ghost 4

'I'm certainly happy to have done it, and I've met some terrific people through ghosting, and heard some wonderful stories from people it has been an honour to meet.'

Zoe King

'I'm proud of everything I write, but was particularly pleased with the first couple of chapters of Never Say Die, simply because it was the first time I'd attempted to meld my storytelling and writing skills with someone else's true life experiences, in such a way that was both diplomatic (expunging or radically altering another person's words is never easy!) and made the subject feel that thrill of recognition. People often say that as soon as they start reading Never Say Die they can't put it down, and I find that really satisfying.'

Lynne Barrett-Lee

Points to remember

- Celebrate when any project is completed.
- When the actual book is delivered, put yourself into your client's shoes for the final time. Feel their excitement.

- Ghosts can choose whether to be involved in the sales and promotion of clients' work.
- Ghostwriters can advise on the next step for the client— selling and promoting.
- Now is the time to look for your next project, unless you already have one.

12 Ethics

A good read

The whole concept of ghostwriting could be said to be on shaky ground when it comes to the moral side of things. Are we, as ghostwriters, duping the public into thinking that the book they are reading has actually been written by the person whose name is on the cover? That thought alone might be enough to put some writers off ghosting. But who would write that person's story if there wasn't a ghostwriter willing to take on the job? The answer is no-one. The story would be lost. Or the subject might have a go at it themselves, their story would be told badly and because of that it wouldn't be read.

One opinion is that a good read is a good read whoever the words are credited to.

If we were to discover that our favourite author had only ever come up with a slight idea for a plot and a couple of characters, then someone totally unknown had crafted those tiny pieces into all of his or her best-selling novels, would we stop reading those books?

Can't write, won't write

Painters and decorators can turn a dreary living room into something inviting, or even spectacular. We are capable of having a go at doing it ourselves but don't have the time, or the skills. The finished product wouldn't be as good.

Ghostwriters provide the same sort of service. They write for the people who cannot put their stories into words for themselves, or the ones who don't even want to try but do want to see a book with their name on and know that it has been well done.

Ghosting for celebrities

Is ghostwriting novels for famous names ethical? The books put money into the pockets of ghostwriter, star and publisher alike. And, considering the huge numbers that are bought, the general public are happy too. With so much money involved could you afford to say no to ghosting a footballer's autobiography or a novel that is going to have the name of a top model or soap star emblazoned across its cover? One opinion was that a big name on a novel would get followers of that name reading when they had been non-readers before. Another opinion is that a badly produced novel, supposedly written by a top celebrity, would put a new reader off novels for good.

Speeches and poems

Is it going to give you sleepless nights if you write the loving vows for a groom to say to his wife on their wedding day? Will you feel guilty at the thought of a young girl reading a love poem on Valentine's Day and thinking her boyfriend has a sensitive side she didn't know about? Wouldn't it be more likely that the recipient of the verse would guess their partner hadn't written it? They'd still be pleased to know they'd gone to the trouble of getting a poem written.

Students

Ghostwriting for students is considered shaky ground. There are internet sites where students can pay a ghost to do their course work and theses for them. They can even tell the ghostwriters what grade they want to get and the ghostwriter will cater for this. Isn't this classed as cheating?

Many writers wouldn't go near any ghosting assignment like this but there are those who do and they are asking for, and getting, good money for doing so. One webpage reported how they covered every field—languages, mathematics, biology, science. They even offered Masters degrees, for a price.

Another point of view is that many students cannot express themselves clearly in writing. They know their subject inside out, can talk about it at length and can perform all the practical aspects of it. They just need help to get all that down in writing so they ask a ghostwriter for help.

To do or not to do

Consider this. Most ghostwriting is a joint effort. Your client has the story and you have the ability to write it for them. I'd call that a partnership.

If you are unsure about any project you are asked to be involved with then you can always say no. But think what you might be missing!

Points to remember

- Ghostwriting is about a writer offering a professional service to a non-writer.
- Your work can help people achieve their dreams and share their stories.
- If your morals are offended then either turn down the job or tackle it by acting like a professional.